A Commitment To Protect

Supervising Sex Offenders: Proposals for More Effective Practice

SOCIAL WORK SERVICES INSPECTORATE FOR SCOTLAND

1997

Purpose and responsibilities

Our purpose is to work with others to continually improve social work services so that:

- they genuinely meet people's needs; and

- the public has confidence in them.

 Corporate member of Plain English Campaign. Committed to clearer communication.

| 27 |

The Social Work Services Inspectorate
James Craig Walk
Edinburgh
EH1 3BA

Secretary of State

I was asked to review arrangements for the supervision of sex offenders. I am pleased to submit this first report. I shall submit a further report in 1998.

The review was set the following terms of reference:

To review the current arrangements for the supervision of sex offenders in the community.

To assess the efficacy of the arrangements and protocols in place for the discharge of sex offenders from prisons and other institutions.

To review the arrangements for accommodation, treatment and monitoring of sex offenders in the community.

To make recommendations.

Angus Skinner
Chief Social Work Inspector

Preface

Some commentators suggest that the concern about sex offending over recent years and months reflects a form of 'moral panic', a preoccupying worry about a particular issue which sweeps across society and then abates. At times it has, for some, seemed as if the problems are beyond reasoned response, and this has sometimes ended in tragedy for innocent casualties.

We do not think that the continuing expression of concern about sex offenders is a moral panic. Rather it reflects a determination that we should find more effective ways of dealing with sex offending to protect communities better. This report makes recommendations to achieve that.

In the first stage, from April–September 1997, we have considered:

- comment and submissions from criminal justice and legal interests, social work, the police, health, housing and education interests, voluntary organisations and others dealing with sex offenders,

- the research and practice literature,

- statistics on sex offending,

- a survey of all community services providing programmes to bring about change in sex offenders' behaviour.

We have visited local authorities, special projects, and initiatives in the community, a prison and one hospital and other agencies and services currently working with sex offenders in Scotland and in England.

Since this review was announced, many agencies, particularly local authorities and the police, have developed or are planning new arrangements, and since the beginning of September all the agencies involved are engaged in implementing the Sex Offenders Act 1997. We have sought to reflect these changes where we can.

The review team comprises SWS Inspectors Ms Stella Perrott and Ms Jackie McRae, Senior Research Officer Ms Sue Morris and Research Assistant Mr Duncan Gourlay. Mr Iain Fitheridge provided administrative support. We are grateful to other colleagues in The Scottish Office for their assistance throughout.

Many organisations and individuals have assisted during the review. We are very grateful for this assistance and hope we have included all in our acknowledgements at the end of this report.

CONTENTS

Contents

Introduction

This Report

1   This first report is an overview of the arrangements for the supervision of sex offenders in the community and a broad assessment of their strengths and weaknesses together with recommendations for improvements. There are four chapters following this brief Introduction. First, an Overview of Sex Offending in Scotland; second, a chapter on Monitoring, Risk Assessment, Supervision and Accommodation; third, a chapter on Treatment and Personal Change Programmes; and in the final chapter we bring together our Conclusions and Recommendations. We make seven recommendations.

2   We have drawn heavily on research studies from Britain and abroad and a review of the literature is at Appendix 1. Details of our survey of community-based change programmes are at Appendix 2.

Related Initiatives

3   Several other initiatives are relevant to the issues considered in this review. We outline them here to show the extent of this related activity and to emphasise that several agencies and systems carry responsibility for public protection.

The Sex Offenders Act 1997

4   This Act requires persons convicted of certain sex offences to register their name and address with the police and to keep the police notified of any changes for a set period of years (the number of years depending on the sentence). This Act was implemented on the 1st September 1997. It plays a significant role in new monitoring arrangements and is discussed further later in this report.

Sex Offenders: Ban on Working with Children

5   A joint Home Office/Scottish Office consultation paper issued in 1996 made proposals which would, if implemented, make it an offence for those convicted of certain offences against children to apply for work which would give them access to children. Responses to this consultation paper are being considered.

Follow-up to the Dunblane Inquiry Report

6   In his report published on 16 October 1996, Lord Cullen recommended establishing a system for the accreditation to a national body of clubs and groups attended by children and young persons under 16 years of age for their recreation, education or development. The main purpose of such a system would be to ensure that there were adequate checks on the suitability of leaders and workers who have substantial unsupervised access to children and young people.

Introduction

7   The Government accepted the recommendation and the Scottish Office issued a consultation paper to relevant bodies about how it may be implemented. The consultation has drawn a large number of responses that are being carefully analysed.

The Police Act 1997

8   When brought into force, Part 1 of this Act will extend access to criminal record information and provide for the release of relevant non-conviction information about people who will have substantial access to children.

9   Under existing arrangements, criminal record checks are available to employers in the public sector who appoint people to positions which will give them substantial access to children. As such positions are exceptions to the Rehabilitation of Offenders Act 1974 (ROA), all convictions including spent convictions are disclosed.

10   Part V of the 1997 Act provides for three types of criminal conviction certificates. The first of these is a criminal conviction certificate which will be issued to any individual who applies to the Scottish Criminal Record Office (SCRO) and will give details of any unspent convictions or state that he or she has no such convictions. The second is a criminal record certificate which will contain details of spent and unspent convictions and will be available only for those occupations which are exemptions to the ROA. The third is an enhanced criminal record certificate that will contain, besides all criminal convictions, information from local police records where this is considered relevant to the post being sought. Initially these enhanced certificates will only be available for those working on a regular unsupervised basis with children. The Act provides for regulations to extend checks to those who work with vulnerable adults and there is a good case for including people employed to care for those with learning disabilities as soon as practicable. Pending the implementation of the Police Act, the government intends to extend existing arrangements applying in the public sector to relevant voluntary child care organisations.

Powers to take DNA samples

11   The Criminal Procedure (Scotland) Act 1995 and the Crime and Punishment (Scotland) Act 1997 introduced new powers for the police to take DNA samples from offenders convicted of sexual or violent offences. This will assist detection and prosecution of sex offenders.

Review of Safeguards for Children Looked After Away from Home

12   In July 1996, Mr Roger Kent CBE was commissioned to conduct this review for Scotland; a similar review was commissioned for England and Wales. Mr Kent has examined measures taken to protect children cared for away from home and assessed whether the safeguards in place are sufficiently effective. His report was published in November 1997 and will be the subject of public consultation.

Victim Notification

13   Victims can ask to be notified when the perpetrator of violent or sexual offences against them is due to be released at the end of their sentence. This applies to offenders given sentences of four years or more imposed from 1st April 1997.

Community Protection Orders

14   The Scottish Office is consulting on the proposed introduction of Community Protection Orders which would prohibit convicted sex offenders from specified activities, such as visiting school playgrounds, making them liable for sanctions up to five years imprisonment if they breached these prohibitions. The order would be applied for either by the police or by a local authority (a point on which the government is consulting).

15   All of these initiatives will strengthen public protection by complementing existing services provided by the police and local authorities. These services include work by the police and social work services in investigating cases of alleged abuse of children, and, with other agencies, putting in place plans to protect children at risk. Collaboration with health and education services are vital to these services, and education also plays an important role in alerting young people to potential dangers.

An Overview of Sex Offending

This chapter describes what is known about sex offending in Scotland and what we may learn from elsewhere. It contains information on the number of sex offences recorded by the police, and on sex offenders and how they are dealt with.

What is sex offending?

1   Sex offending is difficult to define, as well as being complex to deal with. Criminal justice statistics categorise all offences related to sexual activity under the heading 'crimes of indecency'. This category includes a wide range of offences but our concern is with offences involving exploitation or assault. These include rape, sexual assault, homosexual assault, lewd, indecent or libidinous behaviour or practices, shameless indecency, and the possession of pornographic images of children under the age of 16. These offences require convicted sex offenders to register their names and addresses with the police in the area where they live. **This report is about the arrangements for supervision in the community of sex offenders - primarily those convicted of these crimes.**

How is sex offending dealt with?

2   The Courts have powers to deal with sex offenders in a number of ways. Over half of all those convicted of sexual assault and over a third of all offenders convicted of lewd and libidinous practices against children are sent to prison. Other penalties imposed on those convicted of sex offences include probation, community service, admonition, fines and compensation. Courts also determine, with advice from health professionals, whether an offender is suffering from mental disorder. Most sex offenders are not mentally ill: those who are, when convicted and sentenced to custody, may undergo treatment while serving a prison sentence. Mentally disordered offenders who are given a hospital direction may receive treatment in hospital and return to prison once they no longer require treatment. Mentally disordered offenders who are ordered to be detained in hospital by the court may undergo treatment in hospital. In certain cases, a condition of psychiatric treatment in the community may be imposed where the court does not consider a sentence of imprisonment or detention in hospital to be appropriate.

3   Dealing with sex offending is fraught with difficulties. There are difficulties about detection: for instance, low levels of reporting of sex offences. There are difficulties about conviction: for instance, problems with evidence in cases involving sex offences. The police clear up most of the sexual crimes reported to them (clear up rates for sex offences are high compared to other crimes). However, the proportion that proceeds to prosecution appears low compared to other crimes. There are difficulties in trying to change sex offenders' behaviour and dealing with sex offenders after they have completed their sentence can also present difficulties, because of public anxiety.

4   Despite the difficulties, the response to sex offending is strong in a number of important areas. All the agencies involved take the problem very seriously and generally collaborate well. Programmes involving cognitive and behavioural work with sex offenders show some success in reducing reconviction rates for some child sex abusers. The agencies involved,

local authorities, police, voluntary organisations, prisons, and health boards, have a history of co-operation to build on.

What is the extent of sex offending?

5   The largest offence category in 1995 was lewd and libidinous practices (2,381 recorded crimes of which 1118 were offences against children). There were 1,638 recorded crimes of sexual assault (including 403 rapes) and 1,528 other crimes including defilement of under-age girls, incest and homosexual acts. More detailed information on the range of offences included within the category of crimes of indecency is given in the Annex to Appendix 1. This also describes different possible approaches to definition of sex offences and sex offenders.

6   There is no agreed definition of 'serious sex offences'. However, our main interest is in crimes of sexual assault and in lewd and libidinous practices towards children and figures for these crimes in 1985, 1990, and 1995 are in Table 1 below.

Table 1 Recorded crimes of sexual assault and lewd and libidinous practices towards children 1985, 1990 and 1995.[1]

	1985	1990	1995
Sexual Assault			
Recorded crimes	1397	1458	1638
Crimes cleared up	832	974	1077
Clear-up rate	**60%**	**67%**	**66%**
Number of persons proceeded against at Court	226	233	181
Number of persons convicted	148	168	134
Lewd and libidinous practices towards children			
Reported crimes	680	1045	1118
Crimes cleared up	584	909	1010
Clear-up rate	**86%**	**87%**	**90%**
Number of persons taken to Court	182	273	307
Number convicted	156	219	255

Notes: A crime may be committed by more than one person and one person may commit more than one crime. Crimes detected are shown against the year in which they were cleared up and may have been recorded in a previous year. A crime or offence is regarded as being cleared up if one or more offenders was apprehended, cited, warned or traced for it. In relation to court convictions, the crime shown is the crime resulting in the most serious outcome. Thus, there will have been some offenders convicted of other crimes including murder or serious assault who also committed a sexual crime but who are not included in the 'sexual crimes' category.

7   This table shows that over these ten years the number of recorded crimes of sexual assault rose by 17% and the number of crimes of lewd and libidinous practices towards children rose by 64%. If the increase in the number of recorded crimes reflects an increase in crimes committed, then that is concerning. However, rather than an increase in crimes, it may well reflect a greater willingness to report them to the police.

8   There is little doubt that many sexual offences are not reported although it is very difficult to estimate how extensive under-reporting may be. The majority of offences

---

[1] Criminal Justice Statistics, The Scottish Office.

reported, whatever their nature, do not result in conviction and sentence in the courts. The Scottish Crime Survey in 1993 indicated that 61% of all offences were not reported to the police and since sex offending, by its very nature, is secretive and reporting it presents particular difficulties, it is likely the percentage of sex offences not reported is even higher.

9   Table 1 also shows that during this period the percentage of recorded cases of sexual assault that were cleared up rose from 60% to 66% and the percentage of recorded cases of lewd and libidinous acts towards children that were cleared up rose from 86% to 90%. These clear-up rates are already high compared with most crimes and this may reflect the fact that most offenders are known to their victims. The improvement during this period indicates that the public can have confidence in the effectiveness of the police investigation of sexual offences when they are reported to them.

10   This table also shows that, of cases of sexual assault taken to Court, the proportion resulting in a conviction rose from 65% to 74% (though the actual number of cases fell in 1995). Of cases of lewd and libidinous practices towards children taken to Court, the proportion resulting in a conviction remained above 80% throughout.

11   Sexual offences are by their very nature often difficult to investigate and prosecute. Successful prosecution requires corroboration of the victim's evidence which is frequently difficult to obtain. If the victim is a child, she or he may not be able to give evidence fully and there are rarely witnesses to sexual offences. People with learning disabilities need considerable help in understanding what is being asked of them and their slowness of comprehension may undermine confidence in the accuracy of their testimony. These factors may cause a Procurator Fiscal to doubt that a prosecution will succeed.

12   Nonetheless, there are promising signs of progress in both the reporting of crimes and in obtaining convictions. There may be a long way to go, but we should not expect rapid progress in this complex field; indeed attempts to find quick solutions may simply backfire.

What do we know about sex offenders?

13   Almost all convicted sex offenders are men. Of those convicted of sexual assault in Scotland between 1988 and 1995, 670 were men and only 2 were women; of those convicted of lewd and libidinous practices towards children 1,826 were men and 29 were women. This fundamental feature of sex offending must be considered in determining effective policies and programmes to reduce risk.

14   Sex offenders' victims are almost always women and children. Importantly most sexual offences are committed by people known to their victims. Random attacks by strangers are rare. Most of those who offend against children are in positions of responsibility, authority and trust in relation to their child victims and many are fathers and stepfathers. Women too are most likely to be offended against by men they know. Many sex offenders target those least able to protect themselves and therefore public agencies working with children and vulnerable adults must be especially alert to the risks.

15   The peak period for criminal convictions generally is between 15 and 18 years. Once offenders reach their mid-20s there is normally a falling-off in offending, often associated with new stability in relationships, employment and accommodation. The figures for sexual offenders indicate that they are often convicted at a later age and that the peak period for convictions of sex offences is between the age of 25 and 39. This different age profile of sex offenders has important implications for policies and practice. The age spread for

convictions for all crimes, and for serious sex offences (sexual assault and lewd and libidinous practices towards children) are shown in Figure 1 below.

Figure 1 Comparative age distribution of persons convicted of all crimes and persons convicted of sex offences (sexual assault or lewd and libidinous practices towards children) 1988 - 1995.

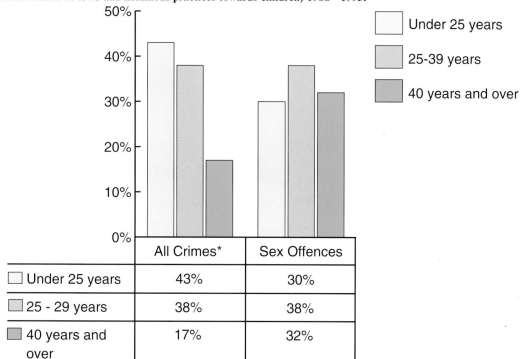

	All Crimes*	Sex Offences
☐ Under 25 years	43%	30%
☐ 25 - 29 years	38%	38%
☐ 40 years and over	17%	32%

* In 2% of cases for all crimes the age of the offender in not known.

16   Sex offenders generally have low rates of re-conviction. However, reconviction rates do not tell the whole story because many crimes are unreported and some sex offenders may subsequently be convicted of other, and perhaps more serious, crimes. It may be, therefore, that some sex offenders are particularly likely to re-offend. The difficulty is how to identify who poses what risk.

17   The picture is complicated by the fact that some offences were committed several years before the offender's eventual conviction (offences against children may only come to light when the victim is an adult). Some sex offenders start offending when they are quite young and later in this report we consider the implications of this. Others may not. A significant number persist into middle age or later.

18   Perceptions of sex offenders have changed over time. Sex offenders are variously viewed as having some physiological or mental disorder which explains their offending behaviour; or as having psychological difficulties which underlie their offences; or as psychopaths who endanger the lives of their victims. Very few sex offenders are diagnosed as having physiological or mental disorders, although psychologists consider that a sizeable proportion have personality problems.

19   Most recent theories of sex offending suggest that sex offenders have cognitive and behavioural dysfunctions that are associated with different types of sex offending. For example, there is strong evidence that the psychological profiles, deviancy levels and offending histories of men who sexually abuse children are different from those of men

who rape and sexually assault adult women. There are, however, differences among offenders within each of these groups and some men rape and abuse adult women and children. Several classification systems have been developed which help in predicting risk, but none has yet been shown to be wholly reliable.

What do we know about young offenders?

20   Knowledge about sex offending by children and young people is still at an early stage of development. For instance, research in progress at Great Ormond Street Hospital explored the characteristics or life experiences of boys who became sexual perpetrators in early adolescence to identify factors that may increase the risk of a young person becoming an abuser. The multi-disciplinary research team assessed groups of boys who were perpetrators of sex offences, some of whom had themselves been victims of sexual abuse and some who had not, and a comparison group of boys who demonstrated other forms of anti-social behaviour. Early findings confirm that family relationships and experiences of abuse may contribute to the development of a tendency towards sex offending in young people. Separation from parents or carers and experience of family violence were common to both victim and non-victim perpetrators of abuse, confirming other findings that separation features in the life of offenders. Other significant factors in perpetrators who had also been victims were witnessing or experiencing intrafamilial violence, rejection by family, and unusual psychiatric symptoms, including pseudo-psychosis and symptoms suggestive of Post Traumatic Stress Disorder. Boys who were not themselves victims appeared more likely to become perpetrators if they lacked a satisfactory father figure, and if their mother had been sexually abused as a child.

What can we tell from child protection?

21   The criminal justice system, which deals with offenders, and the child protection system, which seeks to protect children, are both concerned with preventing sex offences. Children who may be in need of protection from a convicted or suspected abuser may be referred to local authority child protection services and, where appropriate, to a Children's Hearing. The Scottish Office publishes information from the Child Protection Information System (CPIS) which records information about children referred because of suspected abuse or neglect. Regrettably, not all authorities participate in this system. In the following paragraphs we highlight key information for 1994-95[2], the most recent year for which figures are available. Some of the detailed figures exclude the former Grampian, Strathclyde and Tayside Regional Councils. Victims are unlikely to be referred to the child protection system unless they remain at risk from an offender. Therefore, the victims of strangers, or men imprisoned for long periods, are less likely to be included in child protection figures.

22   In 1994–1995 we estimate that there were some 580 children about whom there was sufficient concern that they may have been sexually abused to require an inter-disciplinary case conference to be held to assess the case and decide what action to take.[3] Nearly two-thirds of these (356) were placed on the child protection register.[4] Some of these will have been victims of sexual abuse, others at risk of sexual abuse because another child in their

---

[2] Statistical Bulletin *Child Protection Management Information* 1994–95 (The Scottish Office, 1996).
[3] Based on 517 children recorded in CPIS and 69 estimated pro-rata for Grampian.
[4] Based on 322 recorded in CPIS and 34 estimated pro-rata for Grampian.

household may have been a victim or because an adult in their family or household was a sex offender.

23   Across most of Scotland just under a third of children about whom case conferences were held were under five years old; slightly over a third were aged 5-10 years, and just over a third were in the 11-15 years range. In Strathclyde (which used a different information system), about 20% were under 5 with the numbers of children in the two older age groups evenly divided at around 40%. Children over 15 are not usually referred to the child protection system.

24   Around two thirds of the children referred because of concern about possible sexual abuse were girls, though the proportion of boys and girls about whom a case conference was held are equal. Of all the children referred to the child protection system in the CPIS areas because of sexual abuse, 7% of boys and 7% of girls had learning difficulties.

25   In the areas participating in the CPIS, 256 (95%) suspected perpetrators of sexual abuse were male and 13 (5%) were female. Strathclyde's figures indicated that 17 of 117 suspected perpetrators were female, representing 14%. This percentage appears high. However, information on the perpetrator was missing or not recorded in 22 of the remaining 100 cases therefore complete figures on gender were not available from Strathclyde. Tayside did not breakdown the data by category of abuse.

26   In the CPIS areas 72% of the male suspected perpetrators were related to, or lived in the same household as, the child. Many of the remaining 28% would include men whom their child victim knew, since there would need to be continuing or potential further risk to the child in order for there to be a referral to the child protection system. In Strathclyde, all the recorded male perpetrators were related to the child or living in the child's household as a cohabitee or stepfather. Tayside's data did not break down suspected perpetrators into abuse categories. Grampian did not provide any data on suspected perpetrators.

How is sex offending dealt with elsewhere?

27   In the USA and Canada sex offenders have been treated for some time as a distinct category of offenders and each country has programmes widely available for sex offenders.

28   In Europe, fewer programmes are provided specifically for sex offenders and countries that are seeking to establish programmes are looking to the USA and Canada for models. Eire and Sweden are currently considering police registration for sex offenders, and several European countries including Austria, Belgium, France, Germany and Sweden have recently stepped up efforts against child pornography and abuse. Generally in Europe sex offenders are treated in the same way as other offenders, with decisions on supervision programmes and degree of supervision being determined by the level of risk an offender poses. The Dutch provide for an indeterminate sentence for violent or psychopathic sex offenders and this unique provision is worth further consideration to establish whether it offers a useful model for possible adaptation in Scotland.

29   In Australia and New Zealand registers for offenders against children are being considered. In both these countries unofficial lists including the names and addresses of sex offenders have been published.

The question of public notification

30   None of the submissions we received argued for general notification to communities of information about convicted sex offenders and many argued against it.

31   Public notification of sex offenders released from prison has become common in America and Canada and it is worth reflecting on their experience. Public notification and registration are closely linked.

32   The UK is the first European country to introduce registration requirements for sex offenders. The USA and Canada have longer experience of this (the California registration system was enacted in 1947). In both countries public notification appears to have grown, at least partly, out of problems in the management of the information systems set up to monitor convicted sex offenders.

33   The North American experience shows that registration by itself does not reduce the risk of sex offending; effective management of the information by the relevant agencies is more important. Concerns about the management of the registration systems in the USA grew during the 1980's. One study, by the California Department of Justice, concluded that the accuracy of the addresses was "probably quite poor". In 1984, an attempt to investigate 4,400 registered sex offenders in the Los Angeles area in search of a missing child found that 90% of the addresses were inaccurate. Similar findings in other American States provided the background to increasing calls for public notification of sex offenders. Most states in the USA and at least five Canadian provinces have enacted laws providing for public notification of sex offenders. All US States are now required to establish registers and adopt limited community notification if they are to avoid cutbacks in federal funding.

34   Public notification in North America is still in its infancy and is based on a variety of models, but the evidence to date suggests that it does not succeed in reducing the risk of sex offending. One Washington study found that although offenders subject to community notification tended to be arrested quicker following offences, there was no significant difference between the reconviction rates of offenders subject to public notification and offenders not subject to public notification.

35   Paradoxically, public notification may contribute to sex offenders becoming increasingly hidden. In many American states sex offenders have become increasingly resistant to compliance with registration requirements. Sex offenders are less likely to register if they know that their neighbours will have access to the information. There are implications also for families, friends and relatives of registered sex offenders. The awareness of these implications may reduce the number of victims who feel able to report sex offences against them and increase the trauma associated with reporting. These considerations as well as the dubious efficacy (and ethics) of passing the responsibility for protection against known sex offenders to individual members of society need to be taken into account when formulating policy on dealing with sex offenders. Monitoring and supervision of sex offenders should be handled by public agencies, though the public needs to be informed on how this is done and how well it is done if their confidence is to be retained.

36   The important messages from the American experience so far are that

- sound information management is essential for public protection from sex offenders, and

- public notification does not reduce sex offending.

Conclusion: The Need for Clarity and Collaboration

37   From this general overview of what we know about sex offences and sex offenders, we conclude that two issues are especially important. First, agencies need to be clear about their responsibilities and the responsibilities of others, and that sentencers and the public

need to be clear about how these are being carried out. Second, collaboration between all the agencies involved is central to effective management and reducing risks.

Clarity

38   For all agencies to be clear about their own responsibilities and those of others, there needs to be shared understanding about the meaning of the terms used. Services can only deliver improved public protection if they are well defined and expectations are clear. It is also important that the Courts (and the public) know what to expect.

39   Several submissions to the review rightly called for more precision in the use of key terms. We consider that more precise definitions of 'monitoring', 'supervision', 'personal change programmes' and 'treatment' are essential and propose these below.

40   By **monitoring** we mean;

Routinised arrangements for maintaining up-to-date information about the whereabouts of convicted sex offenders.

The purpose of monitoring is to know where sex offenders are and about their movements.

41   By **supervision** we mean:

Planned arrangements for overseeing sex offenders in the community, designed to manage and reduce the risk posed by the offender within the framework of a statutory order which may be either a community disposal or a post-custodial requirement. The supervision plan includes an assessment of risk and how the supervisor will check on the activities and circumstances of an offender, monitor compliance with all requirements of the order (taking action where necessary) and collaborate with other agencies in managing and reducing risk.

42   Supervision involves assessing risk and putting in place a programme of oversight of the offender designed to minimise the risks. Supervision may take various forms and include checking on accommodation, employment and other activities. This focussed definition of supervision is important in taking forward the changes we consider necessary. Although it does not describe all that social workers do, it will achieve a clearer understanding of the practice of supervision and also make possible clearer description and understanding of their other work in, for instance, personal change programmes.

43   By **treatment** we mean:

Medical, psychological, or psycho-social measures following a medical diagnosis that an offender is suffering from an illness or disability that may be remedied or alleviated by such treatment. In all cases treatment is provided by, or under the direction of, a registered medical practitioner.

44   By **personal change programmes** we mean:

Programmes, including residential programmes, aimed at helping offenders avoid or eradicate their criminal sexual behaviour through control or management of their drives and feelings in other ways than offending. Programmes may use a range of psychological, psycho-social or other methods, and be provided by social workers, psychologists, doctors or other health professionals, and involve others, such as residential or prison staff.

45   There is currently no standard usage or application of these terms. We recognise that adopting these distinctions will have wider implications, certainly for social work services in criminal justice.

Collaboration

46   A Scottish Study published in 1994[5] showed how the history and behaviour of people convicted of sex offences against children varied and changed over time and bore on the responsibilities of several agencies. The researchers surveyed 500 cases and studied in depth 53 men who talked about their offences, background and behaviour. They found that offenders do not neatly fit into categories and that the history of many serious offenders brings them within the fields of responsibility of different agencies in the child protection system and the criminal justice system. A Home Office study[6] concluded that those who presented the greatest risk of re-offending were those who had abused a number of victims, had previous sexual offences, committed offences both inside and outside their own family, against boys and girls and who were themselves abused as children.

47   These and other findings highlight the central importance of agencies working together, pulling together information, identifying those who pose particular risks and co-ordinating plans to reduce the risk of sex offences. The agencies involved recognise this as the quotes that follow demonstrate.

48   The main responsibilities of social workers in the criminal justice system are supervision and the provision of personal change programmes, though they also have some responsibilities for monitoring and may contribute to treatment. In their submission the Association of Directors of Social Work (ADSW) commented on the importance of inter-agency working.

> "[Holding] multi-disciplinary conferences on assessment and risk management is an appropriate approach for these offenders. These conferences should be about the assessment/risk management of the offender and should not be confused with child protection conferences. Agencies to be involved should include social work, police, health, housing, education, state hospital where appropriate and any other agency considered to have a positive contribution to make in the individual case."

49   In this field the police's main responsibility lies with monitoring, particularly with the implementation of the Sex Offenders Act 1997. This involves them in an assessment of risk and in their submission the Association of Chief Police Officers in Scotland (ACPOS) suggested the further development of a partnership approach to this.

> "At present, Offender Services [i.e. Criminal Justice Social Work Services] are required to assess the level and duration of supervision and support given to discharged offenders. There would be merit in creating a partnership approach in this decision-making process to which the police service could add a valuable dimension."

50   The main responsibilities of health service staff are treatment and personal change programmes though as the Royal College of Psychiatrists emphasised "the majority of sex offenders do not have a formal Mental Disorder." The College highlighted the difficulties of "discharging learning disability patients with a history of sex offences ...because of the lack of appropriate facilities", and also emphasised inter-agency collaboration.

> "The need for input by a variety of Health Service professionals (e.g. communication therapists, nurses, occupational therapists, psychiatrists and psychologists) in liaison with Social Services and the Criminal Justice Services, should be recognised."

51   Other local authority services, especially housing and education, also play their parts

[5] Waterhouse, L. Dobash, R. and Carnie, J., *Child Sexual Abusers*, The Scottish Office, 1994.
[6] Beckett, R. et al. *Community-based treatment for Sex Offenders: An Evaluation of Seven Treatment Programmes*, Home Office 1994.

in this field and, as the Chartered Institute of Housing recognises "working with other agencies" is vital and developing.

> "There are a number of local authority areas where agencies are working together and developing schemes and models for the multi-agency assessment of the risk offenders pose to the community. The Institute supports the development of these initiatives and urges local authorities and other housing providers to ensure that they are committed to being part of any initiative. This may mean that in some cases housing departments and their social housing partners make a commitment to reducing the risk dangerous offenders pose by the provision of suitable accommodation."

52   As in other fields, reducing the risk of sex offences may well depend on two things:

√   Professions and agencies being clear about their core responsibilities and delivering on them;

√   Professions and agencies also contributing beyond their core responsibilities to the shared aim of reducing sex offences.

53   Scotland is well placed to develop effective collaborative services because of its size, the establishment of unitary authorities with a strong corporate function across social work, housing and education services, and the opportunities to bring together at strategic and operational levels the work of these authorities with the police, the Prison Service, Children's Hearings and the health services. The fact that at the level of Government policy these responsibilities are held in one department, The Scottish Office, is another advantage. We must ensure we capitalise on these opportunities.

Monitoring, Risk Assessment, Supervision and Accommodation

This chapter begins with consideration of the new arrangements for monitoring introduced by the Sex Offenders Act 1997, early indications of how this is working and of what more may be required to ensure the systems meet the objective of public protection. The second part of the chapter is about the importance of risk assessment which plays a crucial part in decision-making by all the agencies, and the difficulties associated with it. The third part is about supervision, within the terms of the definition we proposed at the end of chapter 1, and how supervision might be strengthened and extended. Finally, we make some comments about the related question of accommodating sex offenders.

Monitoring

1   We define monitoring as:

Routinised arrangements for maintaining up-to-date information about the whereabouts of convicted sex offenders.

2   The Sex Offenders Act 1997 introduces the requirement for people convicted of certain specified sex offences to register with the police in the area in which they live, when they begin a sentence in the community or are released from detention in hospital or after serving a prison sentence. They must register their name, any aliases, their address and, thereafter, any changes to these details. Registration applies for an indefinite period to convicted offenders serving prison sentences, or their equivalent, of more than 30 months and extends for up to 10 years for offenders serving shorter sentences or serving non-custodial sentences. The purpose of registration is to equip the police with accurate information about offenders which will assist the detection or the prevention of crime, and better inform the decisions of professionals responsible for the welfare and protection of children and vulnerable adults.

3   Registration for sex offenders came into force throughout the UK on 1st September 1997. Offenders convicted of new offences after implementation are issued with a certificate by the court in which they are convicted. This informs them of their requirement to register with the police. All the agencies responsible for the care or supervision of offenders currently serving sentences will identify those offenders convicted of relevant offences, explain to them the new requirements under the Act and confirm this information in writing. Agencies will send copies of their written notifications to the local police.

4   Interim Scottish Office guidance on implementing the Act requires police and criminal justice services to agree local arrangements for sharing information about sex offenders who are registered under the Sex Offenders Act. These arrangements must cover the flow of information in both directions. They should include arrangements for the police to share registration information with others when necessary, and arrangements for supervising officers to notify the police of significant changes in registration information about offenders under supervision or known to the service and assessed as posing a risk to others. Whilst it is the responsibility of the offender to inform the police of relevant changes, the public

will expect close co-operation from all those professionals in contact with an offender both to assist the offender to comply with the law, and to share information to enhance public protection.

5   Agencies have been working to get initial registration arrangements up and running smoothly in Scotland as quickly as possible in the first few weeks of implementation. Early indications from police and local authorities are that they managed this satisfactorily. In the longer term the accuracy of information in the system will need to be maintained to a high standard to fulfil its purpose and command public confidence. The police are responsible for the maintenance of registration information but need assistance from other agencies to make sure that it remains reliable.

Maintenance of the system

6   Administrative arrangements for registration have been set up by individual forces. Each of the eight police forces in Scotland retains a record of offenders who have registered locally and passes information to the Scottish Criminal Records Office (SCRO). Some forces also pass information to the UK wide Police National Computer (PNC). A consistent approach across Scotland is urgently required and could, as the police suggest, be developed through the SCRO.

7   In such a system Courts and agencies supervising offenders would send copies of certificates and notifications to their local police force who would record this information and send it to SCRO. When the offender registered, the force would record the information locally and provide information to SCRO, who would copy this to the PNC so that registration had UK-wide coverage. If, 14 days after receiving the first notification, SCRO had not received information confirming the offender has registered, they would alert the force which received the original notification. The police would then make local enquiries to ascertain the offenders whereabouts.

8   Thus there would be a network of information available to all forces, with SCRO at the centre, which would enable tracking of a particular offender over time, and identify which agencies and forces had had previous contact with him. Some approach of this kind is required if the system is to operate reliably. SCRO may require additional resources to establish or manage the system.

Sex offenders not registered under the Act

9   Some sex offenders are not required to register. This occurs in two sets of circumstances which we describe as Type A and Type B cases.

10   In Type A cases, an offender may be charged with a number of offences relating to one incident, and be convicted on the most serious offence. For example, if an offender commits a murder during which he rapes or sexually assaults his victim the Procurator Fiscal may prosecute only the more serious charge of murder or manslaughter and not other charges. A conviction for rape requires an offender to register under the Act; a conviction for murder or culpable homicide does not. Therefore an offender convicted of a murder in which he raped his victim might not be subject to registration on release, whereas an offender convicted of rape alone would.

11   Offenders convicted (after 1st October 1993) of serious charges which do not require them to register but which result in imprisonment for 4 years or more are subject to supervision on release from prison. A conviction for murder means that the offender is

subject to life licence on release. Close collaboration between the supervising authority and the police is essential so that a strategy for monitoring these offenders is in place, whether they have to register with the police or not.

12   Type B cases are those in which there is a sexual element in the crime but this is not reflected in the charge. Certain sexual crimes present particular difficulties of proof because of the legal requirements for corroboration. In some cases the indecent nature of an assault will not be clear from the terms of the charge as there will be insufficient evidence to support that element though the offender may still be convicted of a violent assault. Procurators Fiscal have been provided with guidance about the requirements of the Sex Offenders Act 1997. Where the evidence supports a registerable offence charge and it is in the public interest to prosecute it, Procurators Fiscal will do so.

Verifying information

13   The police have raised the need for adequate powers to verify information provided by offenders when they register. Registration requires the offender to provide details to the police and this can be done in writing. There is no requirement in the Act for offenders to prove that the information they provide is accurate. To provide false information is a criminal offence, carrying a penalty of a fine and/or imprisonment for up to six months. This may deter offenders from providing false information. Nevertheless where the police believe that an offender may have provided false information, or they are concerned that an offender presents a high risk to the community, they should ask the offender to give proof of his address, and the name(s) he uses, for example by producing current utility bills, driving licence or passport, and should take appropriate steps to confirm registration information.

Sharing registration information

14   Interim government guidance to police and local authorities about the Sex Offenders Act sets out the responsibilities of the police in managing and sharing information about high risk offenders to prevent crime and reduce risk. The initial decision about whether to share notification information with anyone outside the police force rests with the police. Not all police officers have access to registration information. Within police forces and other agencies, information should only be shared on a strictly 'need-to-know' basis in order to prevent risk to other people which might arise if access were uncontrolled. Decisions about when to share information more widely must depend on the degree of risk that they assess an offender is likely to pose to children and vulnerable members of the public. These kinds of decisions are taken by senior police officers. The police have to consider the consequences of disclosure of information for other aspects of law and order, and the risk to the community of vigilante activity.

15   The police will not share information with other professionals about every offender registerable under the Act. The police and local authorities will discuss what kind of circumstances and risk may prompt the police to share information with the social work service about an offender who is not already known. To assist this each should appoint liaison officers. However, it is the police who are required to take initial decisions on whether, and how far, to share notification information about an individual and this they must do on a proper consideration of each case.

16   When the police decide to inform the local authority social work service of relevant information about an offender, the social work service will assess the offender's

circumstances and consider with the police what action to take to reduce risk to children or vulnerable adults. In most cases action can be taken without information needing to be shared further. The police or the local authority may persuade the offender to modify behaviour or avoid certain areas or people; an offender under supervision may be returned to court for breach of a condition of his or her order, or recalled to prison if on licence.

17   Again, as with the police, in most cases information about an offender will be shared with a very few, designated professionals in the social work service. There can be no question of wide disclosure and no expectation that staff or Councillors in an authority are entitled to information about registered offenders. Such information must be restricted to those who have a clear role either to supervise the offender, or to take action directly to reduce the risk he or she presents. Where the offender is known to be in contact with children (perhaps as a family member) a case conference including the relevant criminal justice and child protection practitioners will be required. Decisions about when and with whom to share registration information within the local authority should be overseen by the Chief Social Work Officer.

18   Where an offender is believed to present a very high risk the police may decide, in consultation with the relevant social work service staff and with advice from other professionals where appropriate, to give sufficient information about the offender to a third party so that they may take steps to protect vulnerable members of the community. These kinds of decisions must be based on careful assessment of risk, which identifies what the offender may do, and to whom. This assessment should take into account the following factors set out in government guidance:

- the nature and pattern of the offender's previous offending;
- his compliance with previous sentences or court orders;
- any predatory behaviour which may indicate a likelihood that he will reoffend;
- the probability that any further offence will be committed
- the likely harm such behaviour would cause;
- the extent to which potential victims, such as children, are vulnerable;
- the potential consequences of disclosure to the offender and their family; and
- the potential consequences of the disclosure for other aspects of law and order.

19   This assessment requires the police and the social work service to be explicit about the nature and degree of risk from the offender and to consider a range of options for dealing with such risk, so that disclosure to a third party outside the social work service is well thought out and clearly a last resort. Disclosure to a third party, such as head teacher or housing manager, must be supported by advice from the police as to what he or she might do in response to the information given, and about maintaining the confidentiality of the information on a need-to-know basis. The police and the social work service must provide further advice and support as required.

Overview of monitoring to reduce risk

20   Local authorities and police forces already work closely together in dealing with cases of child abuse and neglect. All agencies responsible for child protection contribute jointly to preparation of policies and procedures for handling such cases in their areas, in Child Protection Committees. The guidance encourages local authorities, the police and Child Protection Committees to examine current local arrangements for supervising and working with sex offenders. Some local authorities began this work before the Act was implemented; others are now taking this forward. The Association of Directors of Social Work (ADSW)

confirms that most local authorities have now established liaison systems with the police and that they are creating forums or panels to consider information and decide how to manage risk from sex offending. These forums will involve other services, such as education and housing, and they will consider risk posed by all sex offenders, not just those registered under the Act. They have an important role in harnessing the skills and expertise of local agencies to find ways of tackling risk from sex offenders, to improve public awareness and knowledge about risk, and to work together to make communities safer.

21   The Scottish Office will review the guidance in the light of experience and information from the agencies involved and will issue revised guidance.

22   In the future electronic monitoring may play a significant role in monitoring sex offenders. As the technology develops so will its potential application. Most benefit is therefore likely to be gained by introducing electronic monitoring in ways which complement and enhance the efficacy of other services, rather than as separate systems.

Risk Assessment

23   Risk assessment in work with sex offenders is complex and uncertain. A more co-ordinated and ordered approach will assist the development of better assessments and the developing expertise in specialist prison and hospital services should contribute to further development of risk assessment in community monitoring and supervision.

24   There are several elements to an assessment of risk. We identify four main issues that need to be considered separately and in relation to each other.

- How likely is it that an offender will re-offend?
- If he or she re-offends how serious a crime is he or she likely to commit?
- Are there changes in the offender (for instance his or her mental state) which modify the initial assessment of either of these?
- Are there changes in the offender's circumstances (for instance where or with whom he or she is living) which modify the initial assessment of either of these?

25   Some offenders pose a small risk of re-offending (and many violent offenders are in this group) but if they re-offend then serious harm may result. Some offences such as exhibitionism may not cause as great harm as others, but offenders who commit these sort of offences may be at high risk of persistent re-offending. Some offenders are both persistent and dangerous.

Current Practice

26   The police assess risk when deciding on whether and when other agencies should be informed about a sex offender in the area. Psychiatrists and psychologists assess risk when considering whether to discharge an offender from hospital. Social workers assess risk in work with Schedule 1 offenders (offenders against children), when preparing reports for courts, prisons and the Parole Board, when determining supervision programmes and when making referrals to community resources. The Parole Board assesses risk when considering when to release an offender on licence. The assessments however are frequently informal, not recorded and based on professional judgements without necessarily using the best available tools or research findings.

27   Increasingly organisations involved in the assessment and management of risk, particularly of high risk offenders, favour an inter-agency or multi-agency approach.

Psychologists, social workers and the police assess risk differently and for different purposes. Combining the knowledge of the various disciplines will increase the authority of the information on which decisions are made, particularly whilst the tools available are so imperfect.

28   Social workers are concerned that they do not have sufficient information about offences, both the most recent and previous, to make a proper assessment of the risk an offender poses. Many of the local authority respondents to the review said that they were hampered by a lack of detailed information about offences. Social workers face real problems in making risk assessments if they have only partial information, and it is wholly unsatisfactory if the only source available to the report writer is the offender. Further discussions are urgently required on the practical and policy difficulties that stand in the way of ensuring that social workers preparing reports, at least in serious cases, have good information about current and previous offences. It is not clear how, in Scotland, this may best be done or from what source the information might best come. However, there is a point of consensus that fuller information should be available and The Scottish Office should take forward discussions on this basis.

Risk Assessment Measurement Tools

29   Tools to measure the risk of re-offending have been developed which take account of the key indicators of recidivism. Psychometric tests have been developed to assess attitudinal and behaviour changes thought to be good predictors of future risk, and a number of checklists have been devised to help practitioners assess the risk of serious harm. The Scottish Prison Service is developing a new risk assessment model which will be used extensively within the prison system. A joint Scottish Office/local authority working group is currently preparing risk assessment guidance for local authority criminal justice services. These developments would be enhanced by closer working involving either a joint group or representation from the prison service on the local authority group and vice versa.

30   Risk assessment remains an imperfect science and no one model provides all the answers. The tools that are available, however, provide a framework for structured thinking about the risks an offender poses and the work which should be undertaken to reduce these risks. It is important to establish mechanisms for pulling together knowledge developing in the services (police, local authority, prison and health) so that each can learn from the others. With use the models can be improved.

Developing risk assessment

31   Social workers have a primary role in risk assessment and management yet risk assessments that address the likelihood of re-offending and its potential seriousness are frequently not included in the information provided to courts by social workers at the point of sentence. To do so more regularly would support, rather than undermine, the sentencer's role in determining the sentence required to protect the public from the offender. Without a full risk assessment it is difficult for social workers authoritatively to suggest a course of action to a court that might reduce offending or to alert the court to concerns that indicate it may not be safe for an offender to be released into the community. A full risk assessment is also essential to plan supervision and to ensure that resources are directed where they are most needed so that those offenders who need high levels of supervision receive it. Training will be required for social workers to develop their work in undertaking risk assessment.

32   The purpose of monitoring and community supervision is to reduce the risk of offending and prevent re-offending. This would be assisted by greater formalisation of risk assessments by social workers and by closer working with the police and other agencies. In order to do this effectively it is crucial that those involved in the supervision of offenders have an informed view of the risk the offender poses, the harm that might be caused should there be further offences and what factors should be addressed to reduce the risk. An inter-agency approach to risk assessment has considerable merits. It may not be necessary in all cases and in order to target resources effectively may be better used in high risk cases. In areas where this occurs the quality of information is improved; local knowledge and 'intelligence' keeps supervising officers alert to any emerging concerns, and professional judgements are based more soundly on a thorough analysis of the situation.

33   We consider that formal risk assessment of sex offenders should be undertaken at the following key points:

- in preparing advice to sentencers and the Parole Board;
- in preparing a supervision plan;
- in reviewing that plan at significant stages and at its completion;
- when there is a significant change in an offender's circumstances.

34   The assessment should be based on knowledge of those factors which are known to have the greatest predictive quality, coupled with a thorough assessment of the individual's motivation, circumstances and problems that might impact on any plans to reduce the risk.

35   One review of studies identified a number of factors that seemed of significance in identifying sex offenders at highest risk of committing a further offence.[7] These are not sufficiently reliable that they might be used in isolation but should alert professionals to consider with particular care cases with one or more of these features. Factors identified as strongest predictors of sexual recidivism include:

- a sexual preference for children (in particular for boys);
- a history of sex offences;
- previous sex offences against unrelated children; and, to a lesser extent,
- a history of diverse sex offences.

36   The sharing of information between agencies particularly between the police, Procurators Fiscal, the Scottish Prison Service and social work services, is crucial so that full details of offences and other facts inform the risk assessment.

Supervision

37   In this section we first consider the types of supervision orders, the way courts are currently using these and argue for extending supervision to include more sex offenders for longer periods of supervision. Thereafter we consider how supervision might be strengthened in practice to increase its effectiveness.

---

[7] Based on work by R. K. Hanson from a review of 61 studies. Hanson, R. K. and Bussiere, M. T., (1996) *Predictors of Sexual Offender Recidivism: A meta-analysis*, Public Works and Services of Canada.

Does the range of orders and licences cover what is required and is it sufficiently flexible?

38   Sex offenders may be subject to supervision a) as part of a probation order, or b) on release from prison, or c) under a supervision and treatment order. A range of possible additional requirements may be attached to these orders or licences to meet the particular circumstances of each case. We describe these orders and their use below.

Probation

39   The Court can place an offender under the supervision of the local authority for a period of between 6 months and 3 years. An order can include any requirement which is "conducive to securing the good conduct of the offender or for preventing a repetition of the offence or the commission of a further offence." (Criminal Procedure (Scotland) Act 1995 Sections 228 and 229).

40   Before suggesting a probation order the social worker prepares a report for the Court with an outline supervision plan including any specific conditions required to help prevent future offending. The plan will have been agreed with the offender who must consent to the making of the order and any attached conditions at Court. When an offender is placed on probation the supervising officer will specify the activities that need to be undertaken in the action plan. This will include the frequency of reporting to the supervising officer, the attendance at any group or other offending behaviour programme and how the order will be reviewed.

41   During the first half of the probation order National Standards set by Government require at least weekly contact for the first month and fortnightly thereafter. In the second half of the order the contact may be less frequent but should not be less than monthly. If the action plan identifies a need for close supervision then the contact should be more frequent. It is expected that there will be at least two home visits in the first three months of the order.

42   If an offender does not comply with the requirements of the order, the supervising officer may issue a warning to the offender. If the breach is serious, for example failure to reside at a specified address, or there has been a previous warning, the supervising officer is expected to institute breach proceedings (i.e. to return the offender to Court). If the breach is proved the Court can impose a fine, vary the conditions of the order, impose a community service order in addition to the probation order or terminate the order and sentence the offender for the original offence.

43   We have considered whether the probation order should be longer than the maximum length of three years and conclude that it would be more sensible to increase the use of existing powers before extending powers. As Table 2 below shows, most probation orders are for periods of 2 years or less and the potential to make longer probation orders is, as yet, little used. In 1994 (the most recent year for which figures are available) 97% of all probation orders were for 2 years or less. More use was made of longer probation orders for crimes of indecency, but still only 15% of probation orders made for these crimes were of over 2 years.

Table 2 Length of Probation Orders 1994.[8]

	1 year or less	2 years or less	Over 2 years	Total
Indecency	61 (43%)	59 (42%)	22 (15%)	142
All crimes	2061(58%)	1352 (38%)	142 (4%)	3555

[8] SWSG Statistics. Information on additional 682 cases not available.

44   Although we are not recommending that the probation order should be made longer for sex offenders, this is an area to keep under review.

45   In 1995, 70 sex offenders were sentenced to less than a year in custody and released without supervision into the community. Supervision on a probation order (strengthened in ways we outline later in this report) would offer better protection to the community, particularly if a change programme was made a condition of the order. If greater oversight is needed a condition of residence might be attached to the order.

Supervised Release Orders

46   When sentencing an offender to imprisonment for between one and 4 years the Court may make a supervised release order requiring the offender to undergo supervision on release for a period of not more than 12 months. Supervision cannot extend beyond the date on which the full term of imprisonment elapses (Criminal Procedure (Scotland) Act 1995 Section 219).

47   If the offender is released on a supervised release order and is in breach of the order, the matter must be dealt with by the Court where the order was made. If proven the Court can amend the order, and insert an additional requirement, or can return the offender to prison.

48   This order was introduced in 1993. In the first two years (October 1993 - September 1995) 112 offenders were made subject of supervised release orders, of whom 19 were sex offenders. In each case sentencers ordered the maximum length of supervision available to them. We estimate that during that period about 170 sex offenders were sentenced to imprisonment for between 12 months and 4 years, so only about one out of every nine was made subject to supervision on release. We consider that greater use should be made of supervised release orders in order to reduce the risk posed by sex offenders on their discharge from prison.

Prisoners released on licence

49   Prisoners, including sex offenders, may be released into the community on licence in three ways.

- On parole licence - following a decision on their application by the Parole Board.
- On non-parole licence - after completion of two-thirds of their sentence. This only applies to those sentenced after 1st October 1993 to more than 4 years.
- On life licence - the Secretary of State, with the advice of the Parole Board, may release a prisoner serving a life sentence.

50   Parole licence and non-parole licence apply to prisoners with sentences of specified periods (called determinate sentences). Offenders sentenced **before** 1st October 1993 may be released on parole licence after having served one-third of their sentence or 12 months, whichever is greater (Section 22 of the Prisons (Scotland) Act 1989). They will be supervised in the community until the two-thirds point of the sentence. The supervising officer may recommend that the parole licence should be revoked early and supervision ended. Offenders sentenced to custody before 1st October 1993, who are not granted early release on parole, will be released once they have served two-thirds of their sentence.

51   Offenders sentenced **after** 1 October 1993 may be released on parole licence having served at least half of a sentence of 4 or more years (Section 1(3) of the Criminal Proceedings

(Scotland) Act 1993). Supervision lasts until the sentence expiry date and may be revoked early on the recommendation of the supervising officer.

52   Any prisoner sentenced after 1 October 1993 to a sentence of 4 or more years will be released on non-parole licence on completion of two-thirds of the sentence (Section 1(2) of the Criminal Proceedings Act (Scotland) 1995), if not released earlier on parole licence. Supervision lasts until the sentence expiry date unless the supervising officer recommends that it be ended earlier.

53   Life licence applies to prisoners with sentences without a specified period, or life sentences (called indeterminate sentences). The Secretary of State for Scotland, on the recommendation of the Parole Board and after consultation with the Judiciary, may release on life licence a mandatory life prisoner i.e. anyone convicted of murder (Section 1(4) of the Criminal Proceedings (Scotland) Act 1995). The Secretary of State **must** release on licence a discretionary life prisoner at the direction of the Parole Board if the Board is satisfied that imprisonment is not necessary to protect the public (Section 2(4) of the Criminal Proceedings (Scotland) Act 1995). A life licence lasts for life, although the supervision requirement may be cancelled after a decade or more of trouble-free life in the community.

54   The Secretary of State may release a prisoner on licence on compassionate grounds (Section 3 of the 1995 Criminal Proceedings (Scotland) Act). The licence lasts until half the sentence if the sentence is less than 4 years and to the sentence expiry date if the sentence is 4 years or longer.

55   Offenders released on these types of licence are subject to the same general conditions on their release as those being supervised on a probation order. In addition parolees and non parole licensees may not travel outside Great Britain without permission and other conditions can be inserted into the licence by the Parole Board or the Secretary of State.

56   National Standards require that the supervising officer should see the offender within one working day of release from custody. Thereafter the offender should be seen at least weekly for the first month, at least fortnightly for the second month, and thereafter no less than monthly. A least one home visit per month should take place over the quarter.

57   If an offender re-offends during the parole or non parole licence period the Parole Division of The Scottish Office Home Department (SOHD) must be informed immediately. If the offender breaches any of the licence conditions the supervising officer can warn the offender for minor infringements but must report serious or persistent infringement to the SOHD. If an immediate recall to prison is required the Secretary of State will revoke the parole licence. Normally the case would be referred to the Parole Board for them to decide to recall the offender, take no action or issue a warning.

Release from prison of offenders against children (Schedule 1 Offenders)

58   Where an offender is serving a prison sentence for an offence against children, procedures outlined in the Scottish Office circular **Child Protection: The Imprisonment and Preparation for Release of Offenders Convicted of Offences against Children** apply. Prison based social workers are required to

- assess the future risk the offender poses to children;
- develop an intervention programme to reduce the risk;
- assist prison management in the co-ordination of a range of interventions from

specialists and prison staff, designed to modify, contain or control the offender's behaviour;

- liaise and co-ordinate with others to develop appropriate release plans;
- prepare prisoners for release.

59   The prison based social worker notifies the local social work service of an offender's impending release in the area in which he intends to live. The community service must decide what further enquiries are necessary; for example visiting the home, checking all available information. A case conference will be necessary if a child or children may be at risk from the offender. Where the offender is under statutory supervision on release the supervising officer and child protection colleagues must liaise closely together and the supervising officer must attend at least one pre release meeting.

Other orders

60   A Court may make a Community Service Order requiring any offender over the age of 16 to carry out unpaid work in the community for not less than 80 and not more than 300 hours, under the supervision of the local authority (Section 238 of the Criminal Procedure (Scotland) Act 1995). In these cases the supervision is generally focused on overseeing the work of the offender on community service. In some cases the community service order may be attached to a probation order which allows for more extensive supervision.

Conclusion

61   This is an extensive range of orders with considerable flexibility and we conclude that new types of orders or licences are not required. However, except for offenders released from prison on life licence, all are time limited. The risks posed by some sex offenders extend beyond the periods of supervision currently available.

62   The majority of respondents to our consultation were concerned about the low number of sex offenders (as a proportion of those convicted and sentenced) supervised in the community following a custodial sentence and the short periods for which they were supervised. Many also suggested that extended supervision on release from custody should be compulsory for all sex offenders.

63   Increasingly, public opinion is demanding that more curbs are placed on serious offenders released from prison into the community. Making supervision longer would meet some of this concern, though it cannot guarantee public safety. Some offenders will evade the requirements of any additional supervision imposed following release from prison, despite the best efforts of those charged with their supervision. This group is likely to include some of the most dangerous offenders.

64   The case for the extended supervision of sex offenders on release from prison rests on two factors. First, the life-time profile of sex offenders is different from the general profile for most offenders, with offending behaviour continuing into later years rather than, as for most offenders, reducing. Second, there is evidence that sex offenders may reoffend many years after a previous offence and without offending (or possibly without being convicted) in between. These factors lead to an extended risk posed by sex offenders which could be reduced by the introduction of extended supervision orders of up to ten years.

65   Where supervision following release is imposed, whether under a supervised release order or on licence, it must end when the date of sentence imposed by the courts ends.

Custodial sentence lengths are fixed mainly with regard to the seriousness of the offence and sex offenders may still present a high risk of reoffending even on completion of a long-term, that is 4 years or more, determinate sentence. Courts should be given further options to consider in these cases. In this respect the Dutch provision for reviewable indeterminate sentences is worth further examination than has been possible within the framework for this initial report. As we recommend later, Courts should be able to order supervision of sex offenders for a period of up to 10 years beyond the date at which the determinate sentence ends.

66   One of the difficulties in introducing a new order would be how to ensure it was applicable in appropriate cases. Some of the most serious sex offenders are convicted of crimes outwith the Sex Offenders Act 1997. The number of sex offenders imprisoned for non-sexual crimes is unknown. Extended supervision should be limited to those convicted of serious offences but considerable reliance would be placed on the exercise of discretion by the Court which at sentencing would need to be as well informed as possible on the matter of risk.

67   The resource implications of this could be significant and there remains the possibility that those offenders who constitute the greatest risk to the community, and whom the community will expect to be most closely supervised, would be precisely those who might try to avoid and evade supervision and subsequent enforcement measures. At the very least, however, extended supervision would provide an opportunity to exercise some additional controls over greater numbers of violent and sexual offenders for longer than is currently the case.

68   There is also a case for making more use of existing provision for discretionary life sentences. Some sex offenders should only be released back into the community after careful consideration and subject to lifelong supervision. In high risk cases the imposition of a discretionary life sentence would mean:

- that an offender will not be released until the Parole Board sitting as a tribunal has decided that it is safe to do so; and

- that he or she will be subject to a life licence which allows for lifelong supervision if necessary and immediate recall to custody should there be renewed concerns about public risk.

69   Such sentences would provide a realistic and more flexible framework for managing the exceptionally long-term risks which some sex offenders pose. The nature of supervision would need to be tailored to the circumstances of each case.

Could supervision be strengthened?

70   Criminal justice social work services supervise sex offenders under probation orders, supervised release orders and on licence. National Objectives and Standards have been established for all criminal justice social work services and local authority costs in relation to these are fully reimbursed by The Scottish Office. This provides a secure framework for the effective delivery of the services. Our consultation and observations of practice indicated that in this complex field of work with sex offenders these standards are met and frequently exceeded by local authorities.

71   The supervisors, in consultation with their managers, tailor the form of supervision to each case. A supervision plan is drawn up based on an assessment of the offender, the risk he or she poses and what might be done to reduce the risk of reoffending. The extent or frequency of supervision varies from case to case, though it must never be less than the

requirements set in the National Objectives and Standards. In some cases the supervision is very intensive. In many authorities supervision of sex offenders is regularly undertaken by two social workers working together. Cases are reviewed with managers at appropriate intervals and following significant changes so that the supervision plan may be adjusted appropriately.

72   Complex cases involve arrangements for checking the offender's accommodation, and visiting the home periodically. In some cases the offender is resident in a hostel and the supervisor can receive reports from the hostel. Where more intensive supervision is required local authorities often work with voluntary organisations, such as SACRO, in putting together arrangements which provide more regular surveillance of the offender.

73   In high risk cases, local authorities have made intensive supervision arrangements which in exceptional cases may involve 24-hour supervision. In such cases the local authority needs to recruit additional staff or provide funds for the extended assistance of a voluntary organisation in providing a high degree of close personal supervision. This is justified where the level of risk is particularly high, but it cannot be sustained for lengthy periods. No matter how intensive the supervision arrangements are, there can be no guarantee that an offender will not commit a further offence.

74   Supervisors also work with offenders to reduce the likelihood of their reoffending in two other ways.

- By providing advice and assistance to help them secure practical changes in their circumstances (for example, by assisting them in finding routes to employment).
- By making them face up to their offences and the consequences, and either working directly with them on personal change to stop their offending, or referring them to a separate programme.

75   These are important to the reduction of risk and social workers' core training equips them to undertake this work in addition to the aspects of supervision with which we are mainly concerned in this chapter (i.e. oversight and risk management).

76   An order or licence may be seen to comprise a portfolio of different work including supervision, advice and assistance and personal change programmes, as shown in **Figure 2** below. A few orders may also include treatment.

Figure 2 Offenders on community orders and licences: portfolio of supervision, personal change programme, and advice and assistance.

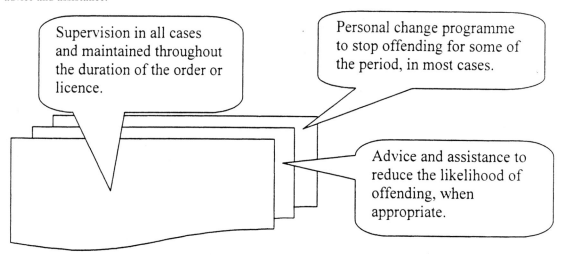

Supervision in all cases and maintained throughout the duration of the order or licence.

Personal change programme to stop offending for some of the period, in most cases.

Advice and assistance to reduce the likelihood of offending, when appropriate.

77 We discuss personal change programmes, and the important role that social workers and others play in these, in the next chapter. They are often considered under the general term 'supervision', but we consider it better to establish a clearer focus on the various separate elements that may be included under an order or licence.

78 Advice and assistance are more integrally connected with the core tasks of supervision and therefore we consider them here. We would emphasise that the purpose of advice and assistance for offenders is to reduce the likelihood of their re-offending and, to that end, to promote their inclusion in society as fully responsible citizens. Offenders are not 'persons in need'. The purpose of supervision is not to provide offenders with advice and assistance but to oversee their compliance with the terms of the order and to adjust the arrangements for supervision in the light of risk assessment. Supervision is about the management of risks posed by offenders in the community.

79 Within this portfolio our definition of supervision is:

Planned arrangements for overseeing sex offenders in the community, designed to manage and reduce the risk posed by the offender within the framework of a statutory order which may be either a community disposal or a post-custodial requirement. The supervision plan includes an assessment of risk and how the supervisor will check on the activities and circumstances of an offender, monitor compliance with all requirements of the order (taking action where necessary) and collaborate with other agencies in managing and reducing risk.

This is not intended to describe all that social workers do within the framework of an order, but to provide for a clear focus, within that order, on what the supervision element will comprise. This is essential in considering long-term supervision orders of up to ten years which clearly cannot comprise constant personal change work or simply prolonged advice and assistance. Clarity of the supervisory element is necessary in all cases.

Practical steps to strengthen supervision

80 The first priority in relation to sex offenders is to consider what practical steps may be taken to strengthen supervision in this sense of oversight. If a high risk offender resides in specialist or approved accommodation, participates in an intensive programme or engages in a schedule of constructive activities this makes the task of supervision a great deal easier, but otherwise the social worker will need to consider other methods.

81 Most social workers could list a range of possibilities for strengthening supervision. The key is to tailor the arrangements to each case and for supervisors to use their creative skills in designing a plan that meets the case and opportunities presented. In this respect social workers should act first as supervision case managers. The specific role they play in the supervision plan may then vary from case to case, but their key responsibilities for risk assessment, for putting in place a supervision plan and for risk management would remain throughout the period of supervision.

82 Some offenders, including some serious offenders, have well ordered lives and a high level of social skills. In other cases the offender may need considerable help with different aspects of his life to establish a degree of stability which is vital to reduce the risk of further offences.

83 Some problems may increase the risk of future offending for example lack of suitable accommodation, employment or constructive activities, mental health problems, or problems with alcohol or drugs. Social workers should provide assistance directly where this is appropriate or help the offender to obtain assistance from other sources. Where

problems have a direct and immediate impact on behaviour, for example failing to take medication, the social worker will need to work with others to ensure appropriate action is taken to solve the problem or institute controls to protect the public, for example a hospital admission.

84   We identified several steps which should be considered in appropriate cases. These are not in general use. The best approach to supervision will always depend on the particular circumstances of the case. Some of the following will be unsuitable in certain circumstances. Social workers should use their skills to design the most effective package for each offender. Most of these elements would need, for various reasons, to be agreed with the offender but that need not limit their effectiveness. To provide an effective service, more of these approaches should be used.

- Requiring the offender to maintain a daily diary of his or her activities with regular checks on the accuracy of the reports.

- A frequent schedule of home visits (including unexpected visits).

- Electronic monitoring of the movements of an offender to check the veracity of their self-reported activity.

- Working with the police in surveillance activities such as monitoring the whereabouts of an offender and his movements.

- Checking house and car for warning signs of increased risk e.g. possession of pictures of unrelated children. Checking with partners where appropriate.

- Telephoning offenders daily (or regularly) to check on their whereabouts and activities.

- Recruiting a 'second report', someone associated with the offender who can report independently on their behaviour and activities. The offender would need to be aware of this arrangement.

- Conducting periodic 'intensive reviews' by monitoring in depth for a short period (perhaps a week) an offender's activities and behaviour.

- Agreeing 'family reports' with an offender and his or her family (including extended family) where they can notify concerns and are interviewed about their perceptions of the offender's progress and current activities.

- Periodic 'intensive assessments', possibly with the offender resident in an appropriate centre for a week, to assess in detail his or her activities, behaviour and responses.

- Unannounced 'report veracity checks' where the details of an offender's reported activities during a supervision reporting session are checked out (with police assistance where appropriate). These may be triggered by unspecified concerns.

- Organising spot checks on offenders under supervision outside office hours where there is particular concern. The police may assist with this as, in appropriate circumstances, could out of hours duty teams.

- Whole day report sessions in which an offender has to report on his or her activities and behaviour in depth in a meeting with the supervisor which lasts all day and during which the supervisor is, if it is a first session, seeking to understand the offender more fully or, if it is a later session, seeking to find out in more depth how the offender is really progressing. These sessions might be run with two staff.

- Observation of offenders in social settings. In some cases this may be difficult to arrange discreetly but such observations will assist the holistic assessment of an offender where they are possible. Offenders are already often observed in group sessions.

- Second observer watching offender reporting to supervisor to better detect manipulative behaviour or evasive answers. Alternatively, video-recording supervision sessions for subsequent detailed analysis of questions and responses (the truth is not always instantly ascertainable).

⚬ Offenders requested to produce documentary back-up of activities.

⚬ More use of 'interrogative' supervision where the supervisor probes answers and statements by the offender to check their accuracy. Social workers' training and their wide knowledge of human circumstances will assist them in this.

⚬ Checking that offenders have activities in the community that will reduce the time they are able to brood on current circumstances and possible future offending.

⚬ "Turn About' supervision where high risk offenders would undergo intensive, close, daily supervision. The intensity of supervision would reduce only as the offender demonstrated increased controls on his behaviour and participation in activities to reduce the likelihood of its occurrence (i.e. was turning about). This form of supervision could be used at the beginning of an order or activated at any time where changes in behaviour or circumstances required it.

When an offender breaches the conditions of his or her order

85   The National Objectives and Standards lay down clear guidelines on action to be taken whenever an offender breaches the conditions of his or her order. Local authorities are putting in place systems for monitoring the adherence to these requirements. In cases involving sex offenders it was clear from our visits and consultation responses that breaches were treated very seriously and appropriate action taken.

86   Where the behaviour of an offender poses such a risk that the supervisor and the police are concerned that harm is imminent, swift action can be taken. Offenders can be arrested and detained (pending a hearing) if they are in breach of their supervision or licence if the Court or Parole Board are satisfied that such measures are needed to protect the public. The framework recently introduced under the Sex Offenders Act 1997, which allows for close working and co-operation between social work services and the police, can be developed further and strengthened to ensure speedy action is taken where necessary.

Making more use of requirements attached to orders

87   The wide potential for attaching additional requirements to probation orders appears not to have been fully exploited in the supervision of sex offenders on probation. These additional requirements, set out in the Criminal Procedure (Scotland) Act 1995, may cover:

⚬ the residence of the offender;

⚬ living in an institution or specified place for a set period of up to 12 months;

⚬ performing unpaid work;

⚬ paying compensation;

⚬ submitting to treatment by, or under the direction of, a medical practitioner or a chartered psychologist.

88   Table 3 below shows how these additional requirements were used in 1994 by the courts for all crimes and for crimes of indecency. It shows that, overall, probation orders made for crimes of indecency were less likely to have an additional requirement attached. Requirements to attend for medical and psychological treatment and to take part in day centre/group programmes were more likely, but not significantly so given the nature of the crimes. There was no difference in the proportion of requirements relating to

accommodation. Greater use could be made of conditions to strengthen the probation order and increase public confidence.

Table 3 Probation orders with requirements attached.

	Crimes of Indecency	All Crimes
No Conditions	72 (49%)	1808 (43%)
Compensation	0	123 (3%)
Residential Accommodation	1 (<1%)	41 (<1%)
Medical/psychological treatment	13 (9%)	123 (3%)
Community service	22 (15%)	1022 (24%)
Day Centre/group programme	18 (12%)	429 (10%)
Drug/Alcohol treatment	8 (5%)	403 (10%)
Other	14 (9%)	288 (7%)
Total	148	4237

89   It is surprising that greater use is not made of the facility to attach appropriate requirements to orders and we consider that social workers, in preparing advice for sentencers on the community supervision of sex offenders, should always consider recommending suitable additional requirements. Requirements to participate in treatment or personal change programmes might be combined with requirements to have no contact with victims or their families, no direct contact with children, no visits to parks, schools, playgrounds, swimming pools, day care centres, or places where children congregate. In some cases the requirements might relate to the possession of pornographic material or other matters.

Developing a partnership with the prison service

90   Community criminal justice services and the prison service share the common objective of reducing offending and there would be considerable benefit from developing a stronger partnership approach in their work.

91   Community supervision of high risk cases (and where possible more generally) should be seen as a continuum which starts from the preparation of the Court report and the first risk assessment, continuing through the prison sentence and after release. Throughout the process, the supervising officer should be informed of the offender's progress and begin to prepare for supervision following release. At present many offenders are not allocated a community supervisor until just prior to release. This means that the knowledge of the offender and the risk they pose is limited; the offender is less likely to engage constructively with a supervising officer who is unknown and has shown little interest hitherto; and there may be insufficient time to make plans that meet both the needs of the offender and reduce risk.

Linking supervision to risk assessment

92   Discussions with staff and managers during the review indicated that there were tensions between the need to supervise according to the risk posed by an offender and the need to ensure that scarce resources were spread wisely and shared between as many offenders as possible. Some social workers are discouraged from intensive work as the order nears completion regardless of the risk posed. The length of time offenders have been on supervision is not an indictor of the level of risk and high priority should be given to those offenders who pose the greatest risk.

93   When the risk from an offender reduces, the level of supervision should be reduced accordingly. Some serious offenders may be supervised for long periods of time and, as we recommend later, this could be extended in some cases to up to ten years. In these cases periodic reviews should be thorough and include a comprehensive risk assessment and checks on the offender's living arrangements and activities, with evidence of them sought where appropriate. Information should be sought from the police and others who may have knowledge of the offender. If all is well then the reduced level of supervision can be continued but arrangements need to be in place to re-activate a higher degree of supervision should it be necessary. At all times the supervisor will need to be alert to any concerns that are raised about the offender or any changes in circumstances.

94   Effective risk management includes the following elements

- oversight and controls based on an assessment of risk;

- reducing the opportunities for offending where practicable (e.g. not being housed close to a primary school);

- systems and arrangements for taking action to protect the public should the level of risk increase to an unacceptable level;

- arrangements to share information as appropriate;

- back-up arrangements;

- regular reviews of risks posed and further intervention planned.

95   The social worker has a clear case management role in undertaking these tasks. They will need to be responsible for the risk assessment and take a lead on managing risk. They will need to be responsible for inter-agency co-ordination and the collation of information from various sources. They should also be responsible for ensuring the offender has access to a change programme and other facilities that can reduce risk. To ensure social workers are skilled in the role of case manager, additional training may be required and, as we note in our recommendations, particular attention needs to be paid to the skills needed to undertake a comprehensive risk assessment.

96   The close supervision and monitoring needed for some of the most serious sex offenders would be more appropriately undertaken by staff with different skills. Social work skills are not always required for this role. Training can be provided for non-social work or ancillary staff on identifying risk factors. The employment of different staff to undertake the oversight and monitoring roles would free more expensive social work resources in order that more offenders could be supervised in the community. In some cases, especially those involving extensive supervision arrangements such as those outlined in paragraph 84, the social worker may act as a 'supervision case manager' with responsibility for assessing the risk, determining the supervision plan and reviewing its progress while some of the work within the plan is carried out by others reporting back to the supervision case manager as appropriate.

Accommodation

97   Homeless and highly mobile offenders are very hard to monitor or supervise effectively. They therefore pose a greater risk and the provision of stable accommodation will assist in minimising the risk of offences. Some of the research literature suggests that offenders in unstable circumstances are more likely to commit further offences. Therefore agencies should co-operate to ensure that stable accommodation is available for offenders on discharge.

98   Prison and local authority staff responsible for the resettlement and supervision of sex offenders in the community now identify one of their most difficult tasks as finding somewhere appropriate for homeless prisoners or offenders to live. Some offenders are made homeless as a direct result of their offending. Their families may decide they no longer want the offender in the household, or child protection agencies may require the offender to leave in order to ensure the safety of his children or others. More recently a number of offenders have become homeless as a result of local and media publicity and campaigns for their removal. Local authorities remain responsible for the accommodation and supervision of these offenders and have had considerable difficulty in obtaining alternative accommodation.

99   Social workers at HMP Peterhead, which now comprises the largest prison population of sex offenders in Scotland, described the problems of finding proper accommodation for prisoners approaching release. They told us that local authorities rarely allocate a community social worker to an offender until he had a confirmed parole or release date. Offenders eligible for parole know that they need an appropriate and stable address to be considered for parole. Prisoners are competing for a small number of places in staffed hostels. The number of hostels prepared to accept referrals of sex offenders is reducing and during the last year there were only two in Scotland willing to consider referrals of sex offenders.

100   Understandably, prisoners are discouraged from settling in the locality of the prison from which they have been released and detention in a prison or elsewhere in a local authority area does not establish a local connection with that area under the homelessness legislation. Prison social workers, therefore, are arranging accommodation for the prisoner with little or no knowledge about the area to which he may be returning and they are not in a position to test whether the accommodation is really suitable. Local authority criminal justice services in turn state that they experience problems when an offender is placed in their area with little prior warning or preparation. These concurrent problems would be eased if throughcare planning and provision between prison and local authorities were strengthened to prepare for resettlement of the offender into the community to which he will be released, at an early stage in his sentence, and certainly before he becomes eligible for parole.

101   Housing policies vary from area to area but local authorities have a statutory responsibility under social work legislation to assist released prisoners and they are responsible for their supervision. A new Code of Guidance on Homelessness comes into force on 1st December 1997 and local authorities have a statutory duty to have regard to this code in the exercise of their homelessness functions. The code says that recently discharged prisoners may be vulnerable and, if they are in need of support and assistance and have no-one to provide this, in priority need and eligible for accommodation. It also suggests that local authorities should consider, for prisoners previously living in council housing, such possibilities as allowing them to sublet their house during their sentence, or coming to an agreement under which they give up their tenancy, but are given an equivalent house on release. There may be difficulties in adopting this approach with sex offenders, for example where the offence involved a member of their household or there is local hostility to their return to their particular area. The Code suggests that in such cases an outplacement in another authority's area, with the person's consent, may be the solution. Careful and considered decisions on each case are essential if the risk of sex offences is to be reduced. Rigid policies, such as debarring convicted sex offenders from public housing on the basis that they have made themselves intentionally homeless by their criminal conduct, are likely to increase rather than reduce risk.

102   Very few local authorities have residential resources within their social work service which can appropriately cater for sex offenders. There are a number of sex offenders for whom supervised accommodation on release from prison is the best option in order to manage the risks they pose and to work towards their fuller re-integration. Local authorities need to collaborate on optimising the use of these scarce resources and recognise that in some cases they will be required to fund supervised accommodation outwith their area. Offenders tend to drift to the cities which are also frequently the chosen destination of prisoners released on licence or under supervision. The provision of supervised accommodation for offenders must therefore be planned, funded and utilised on a strategic national basis drawing on strong inter-authority collaboration.

103   Calls for public notification of sex offenders will continue and in some cases when the identity or whereabouts of a sex offender become known, members of the public will take it into their own hands to inform others and sometimes to harass the offender, and possibly officials, until the offender is moved out of their community. No clear rules for handling these difficult situations can be laid down; the police and local authorities must respond to the particular circumstances of each case. Where an offender is moved then the police must be informed (in order to undertake their responsibilities in relation to monitoring) and the appropriate social work service officer must be informed (in order to put in place appropriate arrangements for supervision). This information should be handled on a need-to-know basis. In these circumstances councillors do not generally have a need-to-know as they play no direct role in the supervision and therefore should not be informed of the new address of a sex offender. Where the offender is moved to an address in a different authority the police and nominated social work service officer should be consulted first; again, councillors should not generally be informed.

104   The response of individual members of the public in these situations is understandable. The facts are, however, that sex offenders must be accommodated somewhere and that public notification does not appear, from the American experience, to reduce risk. In developing new approaches to these difficult problems there may be a role for a technique known as deliberative polling which attempts to bring together expert knowledge and the views and feelings of ordinary people in examining how best to handle complex social problems. Several local authorities and the Chartered Institute of Housing have already produced useful policy documents and others are also working on these. It would be useful for all agencies to be directly involved in taking matters forward, with housing issues being given equal attention alongside those of social work and police.

Improving Treatment and Personal Change Programmes

Introduction and definitions

1   The word 'treatment' is widely used to describe the face to face work carried out with sex offenders by professionals, to reduce the likelihood that they will commit further sexual offences. The use of this term implies that sex offending is an illness which, like other forms of illness, might be 'cured'. It is more accurate to describe sex offending as pernicious and compulsive antisocial behaviour which offenders must be helped to change or control. However, some offenders may need treatment for conditions which have a bearing on their offending. Sentencers, and the general public need clear information about who is responsible for different aspects of the management of sex offenders in the community. We distinguish between treatment for sex offenders because of illness or disability, and work to bring about change in their personal attitudes and behaviour through personal change programmes.

2   Our definition of treatment is:

Medical, psychological, or psycho-social measures following a medical diagnosis that an offender is suffering from an illness or disability that may be remedied or alleviated by such treatment. In all cases treatment is provided by, or under the direction of, a registered medical practitioner.

3   Our definition of personal change programmes is:

Programmes, including residential programmes, aimed at helping offenders avoid or eradicate their criminal sexual behaviour through control or management of their drives and feelings in other ways than offending. Programmes may use a range of psychological, psycho-social or other methods, and be provided by social workers, psychologists, doctors or other health professionals, and involve others, such as residential or prison staff.

4   This chapter focuses predominantly on work to bring about change in sex offenders who are supervised in the community, or who are in prison. We begin by outlining the treatment available for sex offenders with a mental illness. We then describe the personal change programmes available in Scotland which are more relevant to our remit. We comment on provision for sex offenders with a learning disability and young people who have committed sex offences, and conclude with comments on improving effectiveness of current provision.

Treatment

5   Treatment may be provided to remedy or alleviate an illness, condition or disability in the offender, to which professionals may attribute a cause of offending or which may have a direct influence on the offender's risk of reoffending. It includes physiological treatments, such as hormone treatment or surgery, treatment for mental illness or learning disability, or drug or alcohol misuse.

Mental Disorder

6   Only a small proportion of sex offenders suffer from a mental disorder. One study puts the rate as low as 8%. Health services have most direct involvement with sex offenders who have a mental disorder or a learning disability. The Royal College of Psychiatrists argue that psychiatrists should not have a significant role in the obligatory supervision of sex offenders other than those who were clearly suffering from a significant and treatable mental disorder. This is likely to be a small number of cases. Of 148 probation orders imposed for crimes of indecency in 1995,[9] only 13 included a condition of medical or psychiatric treatment, and 8 included a condition of treatment for drug or alcohol problems.

7   Mentally Disordered Offenders may be detained in hospital for treatment under section 57 or 58 of the Criminal Procedure (Scotland) Act 1995 or treatment may be provided in the community under a Supervision and Treatment Order, a provision introduced by the Criminal Justice (Scotland) Act 1995 or alternatively on a Guardianship Order. Some mentally ill people who pose a risk to themselves or others may be discharged from hospital under Community Care Orders introduced by the Mental Health (Patients in the Community) Act 1995. These orders, requiring mentally ill people to comply with treatment outside hospital, may include conditions making the person live in, or attend for treatment, education or training at a particular place. A Community Care Order also provides for rapid admission to hospital if the person's mental illness deteriorates. Under the Criminal Procedure (Scotland) Act 1995 the High Court or a Sheriff Court, having received a report from the local authority, may place an offender under a Guardianship Order. There is a small number of people, usually with learning disabilities, who, having committed sexual offences, are placed on a Guardianship Order. The Crime and Punishment (Scotland) Act 1997 introduced a new hospital direction which comes into force on 1st January 1998.

8   The Mental Welfare Commission has a statutory duty to protect persons who may, by reason of mental disorder (defined in the statute as mental illness or mental handicap) be incapable of adequately protecting themselves or their interests. The Commission thus has an interest in the protection of people who may be vulnerable to sexual assault. For example, it is an offence for a man to have unlawful sexual intercourse with a woman with learning disabilities who is protected under the Mental Health (Scotland) Act 1984. The Commission also has an interest in the care and treatment of mentally disordered persons whether in hospital, in local authority or other accommodation, or in their own homes. The Mental Welfare Commission oversees the care and treatment of persons with a mental illness and visits those compulsorily detained including those under Supervision and Treatment Orders.

9   In appropriate cases the Commission's powers include the discharge of patients from liability to detention or guardianship and the revocation of Community Care Orders. The Commission must be notified of all episodes of compulsory detention and Community Care Orders under the terms of the Mental Health (Scotland) Act 1984 and the Criminal Procedure (Scotland) Act 1995.

10   The aim of the Care Programme Approach (CPA) is to ensure that persons with a severe and enduring mental illness, who also have complex health and social care needs, receive care and supervision in the community. CPA was introduced in Scotland in 1992 but implementation has been patchy. Last year The Scottish Office re-issued a government circular encouraging local authorities, health boards and housing authorities to improve

---

[9] Criminal Justice Statistics, The Scottish Office.

arrangements through full implementation of the CPA. The Care Programme Approach is not mandatory.

11 Under CPA arrangements, a mentally ill person should undergo a comprehensive multi-disciplinary and multi-agency assessment of their needs before discharge from hospital. This should include assessment of any risk he may pose to himself, or others in the community. For mentally disordered sex offenders this assessment should include consideration of the likelihood that he may commit a further sex offence. This assessment is the basis for the person's continuing care in the community - his care programme. A designated key-worker will co-ordinate the person's care and all the agencies involved will review progress together at regular intervals. Patients may also be given leave of absence under the supervision of their psychiatrist for up to 12 months.

12 Some sex offenders who are mentally ill or have a learning disability are detained in hospital after a conviction or finding of guilt. When a detained patient has recovered and detention and treatment is no longer necessary for his health or safety or the protection of other persons, the responsible medical officer, the Mental Welfare Commission or a Sheriff may authorise his discharge. Sex offenders discharged from hospitals will not be subject to supervision by criminal justice services as would other offenders on parole or licence.

13 If an offender's detention is subject to restrictions they may be granted leave of absence from hospital only with the consent of the Secretary of State for Scotland. The offender may appeal against detention to a Sheriff, who may order the person's conditional discharge if he or she is satisfied that the offender is no longer suffering from a mental disorder requiring his detention in hospital for treatment and that it is not necessary he should receive such treatment for his health or safety or the protection of other persons. If he or she is also satisfied that it is not appropriate that the person remain liable to recall to hospital for further treatment, the Sheriff may order the person's absolute discharge. The local authority has a statutory duty to provide after-care services for people who are or have been suffering from mental illness. But, unless an offender is subject to the CPA, there may be no automatic oversight of the arrangements for his care and supervision in the community.

14 There is a need to ensure good liaison between hospital and community health services and social work services at an early stage of planning for the discharge of convicted sex offenders detained in hospitals. Circular SWSG 11/94 established arrangements for communication between prison and community social workers before the release from prison of offenders convicted of offences against children. These require assessment of risk the offender may pose and assessment of whether any action is required to protect children and reduce risk. The Circular does not refer to offenders detained in hospital. Nevertheless there is the same need for consideration of risk and measures to reduce this where these are required. Local authorities and health boards should satisfy themselves that they have adequate systems for notifying local authorities of the discharge of sex offenders detained in hospitals, and that proper assessment of risk to children and other vulnerable people underpins arrangements for the person's care and supervision in the community. The Scottish Office should consider the need to issue guidance on the discharge of detained patients who have committed sex offences.

15 Health boards and professionals stated that there is little provision for treatment or special programmes for sex offenders within the NHS. Nevertheless there are some pockets of considerable experience and developing expertise, particularly in the State Hospital, in which high risk offenders with a mental disorder or learning disability are detained, and the forensic service at the Douglas Inch Centre in Glasgow. This experience and expertise needs to be more readily available to other agencies.

16   In response to the need for specialist secure provision for offenders eligible for discharge from the State Hospital, Greater Glasgow Health Board has developed a 4 bedded secure forensic unit for sex offenders with a learning disability, with plans to extend the service in the near future. Edinburgh Healthcare Trust jointly funds a local specialist sex offender project in partnership with the local authority.

Persons who are not amenable to treatment

17   In most cases hospital admission or compulsory treatment is dependent, not only on a diagnosis of mental disorder, but also whether the patient is deemed to be treatable. This frequently excludes people who have a personality or psychopathic disorder, who are less likely to be amenable to treatment. Professionals from all disciplines find this group particularly difficult to deal with. In addition some offenders may complete treatment for their mental disorder and be discharged, or after a period of treatment be diagnosed as no longer treatable, yet remain a significant risk to others.

18   Discretionary life sentences provide one means of dealing with dangerous psychopathic offenders. However, they do not provide an answer in every case. Some serious sex offenders present a complex range of difficulties only partially addressed by psychiatric treatment. In these cases courts should have the option of committing the offender for treatment within an indeterminate sentence and reviewing the sentence on completion of the treatment. The option of continued detention with or without treatment needs to be considered.

19   When there is little prospect that treatment or personal change programmes will bring about change in an offender living in the community, the main task for local authorities and the police must be to ensure good arrangements for monitoring and supervision with reference to their responsibilities for crime prevention and public safety. In these circumstances health professionals may be required to contribute information as to whether or not the person is likely to pose a risk to children or vulnerable adults.

Personal Change Programmes

20   Most personal change programmes start from the premise that a sex offender must accept full responsibility for his behaviour if he is to learn to control that behaviour. They use a range of techniques and tools to change how the offender thinks about his offence, help him to understand and appreciate his victim's feelings and experience, and find alternative ways of behaving.

21   All of the programmes in operation in Scotland are derived from cognitive-behavioural models which explain sex offending as a cycle with a number of stages, each bringing an offender closer to the point of committing an offence. These programmes are designed to teach the offender to identify his own thinking and behaviour at each stage in the offending cycle and choose to behave differently. Many offenders have little understanding or sympathy for their victims. Many have poor social skills and lack understanding of relationships or sex. And often they are ignorant of basic sexual development and functioning.

The content of change programmes

22   The format and content of most change programmes for sex offenders in Scotland have been adapted from programmes in use in the United States or Canada. They have some, or all, of the following aims:

- reduction in offenders' denial and minimisation of sex offences;

- change in offenders' distorted thinking about sexuality;

- an increase in offenders' understanding of the impact of sexual offending on their victims;

- improvement in offenders' social skills, an increase in self-esteem, and ability to form healthy adult relationships;

- better information and education for offenders about sex;

- change in abnormal or deviant sexual fantasies;

- relapse prevention - finding ways for the offender to avoid situations in which he is likely to commit sexual offences.

Existing change programmes for adult sex offenders

Programmes in the community

23   Most community-based programmes for sex offenders in Scotland are delivered by social workers in local authority criminal justice services or in special projects for sex offenders. We conducted a survey of change programmes and received information about 20 community-based programmes (see Appendix 2). In addition we visited specialist projects and criminal justice teams providing sex offender programmes and talked with staff and offenders about this work.

24   All of the Scottish programmes have developed recently, within the last six years, in many cases because individual social workers identified a need for a programme for sex offenders in their area, and had developed an interest, and skills, in this kind of work.

25   Almost two thirds of adult offenders attending community programmes in Scotland did so as part of a sentence or order imposed by a criminal Court. Staff generally believe that offenders require a conviction and sentence to participate with any commitment. Offenders attending programmes told us that they had agreed to attend programmes to avoid custody, or obtain parole or contact with their children.

26   Change programmes vary widely in length, from a minimum of less than 20 hours to over 150 hours. Our survey found that all the programmes employ some form of cognitive-behavioural method and many are organised around modular courses with a set number of sessions and core content. For example, one of the largest sex offender programmes comprises a three month induction period of individual contact with the offender, followed by 2 phases of group work. Phase 1 is made up of 6 modules each lasting four weeks delivered over a 6 month period, and can be repeated if need be. Phase 2 is designed to equip the offender with skills to avoid reoffending.

27   Most programmes require weekly contact with offenders, although some have more frequent contact, with offenders attending a weekly group and seeing co-workers on an individual basis, as well as attending appointments with their supervising officer. The majority of community-based programmes use two workers for one offender, and programmes work with sex offenders individually or in small groups, or both. Many also work with offenders' families, for example to help them decide upon ways of helping the offender to avoid offending.

Other programmes

Programmes in prisons

28   The Scottish Prison Service (SPS) has prioritised sex offender programmes as one of four development areas for initiatives to tackle offending behaviour. SPS is reviewing the four programmes for sex offenders already in place at HMPs Peterhead, Barlinnie, Perth and Shotts and new programmes for young offenders at Polmont and Dumfries. The most effective elements of each will be brought together in a core programme for introduction throughout Scottish prisons, although the main part of the programme will be centred in the designated specialist halls currently providing the STOP programme at HMP Peterhead. Prisoners will undergo assessment and preparatory programmes at receiving prisons and relapse prevention programmes in the prisons to which they are transferred after completion of the STOP programme. Prison staff and offenders stated that the environment of mutual respect and open communication in the halls in which sex offender programmes are run at HMP Peterhead is one of the main incentives to offenders' participation. This supportive environment is also essential to maintain the observable change in the offenders who attend the groups. It is mainly those serving sentences of over four years who are offered the chance to attend a change programme in prison, but some short term prisoners serving sentences for sex offending also have opportunities to address their offending behaviour. SPS also intend to widen access in the longer term.

29   SPS plan to improve evaluation of prison based sex offender programmes, by introducing pre- and post-programme psychometric testing and ensuring programme integrity across the prisons providing the service. There is a need for greater links between the Scottish Prison Service prison-wide programme and community-based programmes to make sure that both complement and reinforce the other.

Residential

30   Some sex offenders are assessed as needing an intensive residential programme, combined with close observation and supervision, outside prison. The only resource of this kind in the UK is the Wolvercote Clinic, in England. This centre provides residential assessment and treatment programmes for men, aged 20 or over, who sexually abuse children. Some of the Clinic's residents are on community sentences or on parole. Others attend at the request of Social Services Departments or civil Courts where there are concerns about the welfare of their own children, but they may not have convictions.

31   The Clinic is located in extensive hospital grounds, some miles away from any housing, and is surrounded by a high wooden fence with an alarmed gate. The level of supervision and observation of offenders resident at Wolvercote is much higher than that possible for men attending programmes whilst living at home or in hostels, and appears higher even than that for men in prison. Offenders undergoing programmes at Wolvercote felt that the intensity of this programme had forced them to examine their behaviour when attendance at other programmes in prisons and non-residential projects had failed.

32   A small number of men from Scotland have been placed at Wolvercote Clinic, funded by The Scottish Office. A number of submissions argued that Scotland needs its own national residential facility.

33   We consider that there is a case for a residential programme in Scotland, to which local authorities and the Scottish Prison Service might have shared access for residential assessment and personal change programmes for offenders. This might be a community provision which could be used by SPS for pre-release programmes or to assist in the

assessment for parole. It might be a prison unit of a special form and used also by local authorities to provide programmes for offenders serving community services. It might be run by an independent sector organisation and used by local authorities, SPS and possibly health services. It could take a number of forms. The key elements would be that both agencies could contribute expertise through joint management and funding of the service, and its operation would inform, and be informed by, the development of other community and prison-based programmes.

34   In our view there is at present too great a separation of operations between prisons and criminal justice social work services, with little contribution of each to the management of risk presented by sex offenders in the other setting. Personal change programmes provided by different agencies, in settings with different degrees of security and supervision should not be perceived, as they too often are at present, as services for separate purposes. They reflect the broad spectrum of sex offenders and their requirements for personal change programmes. They should, therefore, form a continuum of work with the overall aim of reducing sex offences. This demands much greater communication between the Scottish Prison Service and local authorities in developing change programmes in their respective settings that are consistent with, and will consolidate, work undertaken elsewhere. The residential service could be a key resource within this continuum of personal change programmes and therefore requires the direct involvement of, and oversight by, both agencies. Expertise can be spread throughout the programme continuum by prison and local authority staff being seconded to practice in such a residential programme. Other agencies, health services and voluntary organisations, involved in work with sex offenders may also have an interest in exchange of experience and skills.

The role of clinical psychologists

35   Psychologists have a central role in the assessment and management of sex offenders, and the evaluation of programme effectiveness, in hospitals, other health settings and in prisons. They work less frequently with local authority criminal justice services, although there are examples of successful joint work such as one project where a clinical psychologist is employed partly by the health service and partly by the local authority. Local authorities have traditionally made less use of psychology, and other disciplines within social work services. Our comments, about the need for agencies such as local authorities and the prison service to work collaboratively across traditional divides, apply equally to professional disciplines. Staff working in programmes which employ different disciplines working alongside each other find the mix of different professional perspectives and knowledge strengthens their own practice. No one professional group has a monopoly on knowledge about effective management of sex offenders. To develop their work with offenders effectively, local authorities, in consultation with The Scottish Office, will need to re-examine the mix of skills and expertise within criminal justice services, and appoint more psychologists to assist in the design and delivery of research based personal change programmes. Evaluation should be built in to the management of community criminal justice services.

Provision for women offenders

36   Very few women are convicted of sexual offences. We did not find any programmes designed specifically for women. Only one of the change programmes in operation in the community said that their programme was unsuitable for women offenders. But only two

of the programmes had worked with a woman. Both said that it would not be appropriate for a female offender to participate in a group with male offenders.

Adult sex offenders with learning disabilities

37   Current community based programmes are rarely suitable for people with a significant learning disability. The majority of projects will try to offer an adapted programme for offenders with a mild learning disability, but those that have undertaken this are not confident that this works well. Adaptation of programmes is more likely to be successful when based on the knowledge and skills of specialist practitioners in the learning disability field. Although small scale, this kind of expertise does exist.

38   Offenders with a learning disability are more likely to be diverted from prosecution and less likely to be convicted and sentenced for sex offences. Health services are more likely to take a lead role in supervising and managing risk presented by this group. In some circumstances services reported having to manage offenders who present high levels of risk without any formal legislative framework for the control of their movements and behaviour. Community Learning Disability Teams, where these exist, are more likely to maintain contact with, and provide support for people with learning disabilities for lengthy periods. Submissions from Greater Glasgow NHS Trust Learning Disabilities Division and from the Royal College of Psychiatrists pointed to the movement towards fewer hospital admissions, greater independence and increased placement in the community for adults with learning disabilities. They argue that the level of support and supervision provided for offenders with learning disabilities has in the past been high enough to reduce opportunities for these offenders to commit further offences. Changes brought about through a greater focus on community based care may change this pattern over time.

39   One service discharging long stay patients into the community has introduced a model of working, advocated in a recent report,[10] which appoints a 'risk manager' for each patient to co-ordinate assessment of the risk he poses, identify proper safeguards to reduce risk, monitor how these are working and review them regularly with the other professionals involved. This is consistent with the Care Programme Approach which is also applicable to proper planning for the care and supervision of sex offenders with a learning disability who are being discharged from hospital. The current Circular of guidance on CPA does not refer to adults with a learning disability. We think they should be considered for this model.

Provision for Young Sex Offenders

40   Sexual offending by adolescents can be a precursor to sexual offending in adulthood. Many adult offenders report that they began to abuse children when they themselves were children or adolescents. Unlike other forms of criminal or delinquent activity, young people appear less likely to grow out of sex offending as they mature. Child care professionals are unlikely now to dismiss sex offending by young people as experimentation. Local authority social work services are putting in place strategies to assess and manage the risks presented by young people who abuse others.

---

[10] Churchill J, Craft A and Horrocks C (1997) *There Are No Easy Answers - the provision of continuing care and treatment to adults with learning disabilities who sexually abuse others.* ARC & NAPSAC, Chesterfield and Nottingham.

41   Given their developmental immaturity and, sometimes, vulnerability, the emphasis of work with young offenders must be different to that with adults. Change programmes should include a focus on their psychological and social circumstances to help them achieve healthy adult development, and counteract risk factors relating to psychological and social disadvantage.

Monitoring and Supervision of young sex offenders

42   Whether a young sex offender can be looked after safely at home requires careful assessment. If the young person remains at home his parents or other adults caring for him are likely to need advice and help to supervise and manage his behaviour. Evaluation of change programmes for young offenders is also in the early stages of development in Scotland. One preliminary study of a project in development found a high degree of disturbance and abuse within the families of most of the young people studied, including parents or other adults in the family who had been abused or were themselves abusers, child neglect and significant material problems, such as poverty and homelessness. Although the very small numbers in this study prohibit conclusions, similar high levels of family pathology are reported in studies of the life histories of adult offenders.

43   Children who cannot stay at home, either because they are unsafe, or because their families have rejected them, are looked after by the local authority in foster or residential care. There is concern that children are sexually abused by their peers in children's homes and residential schools. Any decision to place a child who has sexually offended in local authority accommodation must take into account any risk to other children, the level of supervision foster carers or residential staff can provide and the need for a clear strategy to prevent opportunities for the young person to abuse other residents. The Scottish Office and local authorities are piloting new and more comprehensive materials to assist assessment and planning for children called "Looking After Children." These contain specific questions about sexual development and which should ensure that any sexual difficulties amongst children who are looked after are identified and receive attention. It is imperative that sexualised behaviour or sexual aggression displayed by young people looked after is taken seriously and that residential workers and social workers co-operate in work to change such behaviour and manage risk. They will need training and management support in undertaking this. It is not always feasible to place young people who have abused separately from children who have been abused and in any event research indicates that these groups overlap. In response to the recommendation in the report of the residential child care review *Another Kind Of Home*, the Centre for Residential Child Care produced guidelines on caring for young people who sexually abuse others. This is a good starting point for agencies to consider their own practice and management in such cases.

44   Foster carers and any other children they look after, including their own, will need careful preparation for the placement of a child prone to sexually abuse others, and clear information about any previous instances of abuse and potential future risk. All carers of these children, including parents, need good systems of support backed up with training in how to tackle abusive behaviour. Teachers also need to be informed and knowledgeable about how to handle sensitively a young person who may offend against a peer or younger child in school or the wider community.

45   Two specialist projects in Scotland have been set up within the last four years to tackle sexual abuse of children by young people. One project, based in Dundee and serving the unitary authorities in the former Tayside region, is funded jointly by The Scottish Office and a national voluntary organisation. The other is run by Glasgow City Council social

work department, and works with young people looked after by the local authority who have committed sexual offences. Each uses a cognitive-behavioural approach which is consistent with that used in programmes for adults but has been adapted to take account of the developmental stages and the emotional and social well-being of the young offender.

Provision for children convicted of serious offences

46 Establishing the incidence of serious sex offending amongst young people is beset by similar difficulties to those we encountered with adult offenders. However the statistics we do have give some indication of the problem.

47 Most children under 15 who commit offences are dealt with in the Children's Hearing system. Statistics from two thirds of Scotland, including Glasgow, Stirling and Aberdeen, for 1995 and 1996 indicate that, across Scotland each year, the Children's Hearing system dealt with nearly three hundred referrals related to allegations of sexual offences committed by children. These offences included indecent assault, lewd and libidinous practices, incest and rape. (We have not included prostitution and related offences.) The figures reflect the number of offences referred, not the number of offences committed, or the number of children involved. Reporters and Hearings discharge some offences because of lack of evidence. Some children commit more than one offence.

48 Young people convicted in the criminal Courts are likely to have committed serious offences. In the period from 1985 to 1995, 750 young people aged under 18 years were convicted for offences of indecency, excluding offences related to prostitution and procurement of homosexual offences. Forty-eight children under 16 were convicted of crimes of indecency between 1985-95 (including 10 in 1985). Just under half of these children (44%) were sentenced to custody which most will have served in a secure children's home. Fewer convicted 16 and 17 year olds (14%) are sent to custody with 64% receiving probation, community service orders or fines, with the largest number being placed on probation.[11]

49 Children who have committed serious sex offences may be sent to secure accommodation after conviction, or after disposal by a Children's Hearing. Individual programmes including counselling, education and personal development work for individual young people may be arranged but there are no specific personal change programmes provided for young sex offenders in the three national secure units. Secure unit staff lack sufficient expertise and training to run specialist programmes.

50 There is a need for consistent access to skilled work to bring about change for young people in secure care. There will be an opportunity to tackle these problems during the redevelopment of St Mary's Kenmure in the west of Scotland. This unit will comprise five discrete living units within the building. One of these could accommodate young people who have committed sexual offences. This would enable a staff group to develop the knowledge and skills to provide change programmes for young people at risk of continuing to offend in adulthood.

Improving effectiveness of personal change programmes

51 Participation in a personal change programme should be identified as a distinct activity, separate from arrangements for monitoring, treatment and supervision of an offender.

---

[11] Criminal Justice Statistics, The Scottish Office.

52   Research in the UK and the United States lends support to personal change programmes which use a range of methods based on a core of cognitive-behavioural work. Programmes need to be constructed in different ways to tackle different kinds of offending effectively. Programmes should be tailored to individual offenders' needs depending on the risks they pose, the nature of their offending and their abilities. Short focused community based programmes can bring about improvement in sex offenders on psychological test measures. Much longer and more intensive programmes are needed for highly deviant offenders. Cognitive behavioural programmes need careful adaptation if they are to be suitable for offenders with a learning disability.

53   Working with offenders in small groups assists challenging their minimisation and denial of offences, and a group can provide support for offenders to change. Effective groups are those which are well-organised by skilled staff, have explicit rules about expectations and behaviour, and treat offenders with courtesy, giving them respect and encouragement.

54   There has not been systematic evaluation of the majority of programmes in Scotland. As agencies begin to consolidate their work, more work is needed to identify the effects of programmes upon offenders.

55   All the agencies providing change programmes for sex offenders stressed the need for accurate and comprehensive information about an offender's offence. However, in Scotland criminal justice agencies and treatment providers are not given access to witness statements and evidence, unlike those in England and Wales. This hampers credible assessment of the offender and the risk he poses to others. The Crown Office should reconsider how offence information is managed and shared with agencies responsible for the supervision of sex offenders.

56   All sex offenders under supervision in the community should have access to a personal change programme. This will require careful husbandry of the existing knowledge and skills throughout Scotland, and work across agency and authority boundaries. This is already happening successfully in some areas. Specialist projects in the major cities work jointly with local authority social workers to extend awareness and skills outside their immediate operation.

Conclusions and Recommendations

Our main conclusions are set out below.

- Sex offending cannot be eradicated, but further steps can and should be taken to reduce the risk of sex offences.

- Strategic and operational collaboration between the agencies involved should be improved at national and local levels.

- Now that registration has been put in place the professionals responsible must manage information about sex offenders carefully to minimise risk. The public needs to be informed about how information is shared between agencies, and how well, in order to retain their confidence in the systems.

- Additional statutory orders are necessary to monitor serious sex offenders who are not covered by the Sex Offenders Act 1997.

- More use should be made of existing sentencing options. For example, more use should be made of supervised release orders, of longer probation orders (beyond two years), and of the capacity to attach additional requirements to these orders.

- Some sex offenders should be supervised for extended periods of up to ten years or longer.

- Supervision practice should be strengthened to include more rigorous oversight of offenders' activities.

- Assessing risk - though complex and uncertain - is vital, both at the beginning of, and during, an order. Supervision plans should be based on systematic risk assessments, which should be written down.

- Clear distinctions should be made between monitoring, supervision, treatment and personal change programmes so that sentencers, offenders and agencies can be more certain of the implications of different orders and plans.

- The skill-mix in local authority criminal justice services should be developed with the deployment of a wider range of professionals, including psychologists.

- A Scottish residential facility for adult sex offenders may be necessary. This might be especially useful if jointly funded and used by local authorities and the Scottish Prison Service as part of a stronger partnership in tackling offending behaviour. It might be run by an independent sector organisation.

- Specialist residential provision for young sex offenders within secure units should be urgently considered.

- Decisions about accommodation for sex offenders must be made on the basis of each individual's circumstances, taking account of the importance of keeping track of offenders and local public concerns. An inflexible approach may well increase rather than decrease risk.

- Very few men are sex offenders, but almost all sex offenders are men.

- Improvements will require training initiatives, further investment in research and the application of research findings in practice.

Conclusions and Recommendations

We make seven recommendations in order to take forward action arising from these conclusions.

Making fuller use of existing sentences

Recommendation 1

The Scottish Office should consult judicial, local authority and other interests to determine ways in which fuller use could be made of existing sentencing options with a view to

- **making greater use of supervised release orders**

- **making greater use of additional requirements attached to probation orders**

- **providing for a report to the sentencing Court after completion of community-based personal change programmes**

- **making greater use of discretionary life sentences**

- **determining the length of supervision and probation orders in relation to the risk of re-offending.**

The Scottish Office should also consult on how to ensure those preparing reports for sentencers have adequate information on current and previous offences.

1   The well established probation order, and the more recent supervised release order, together provide a steady and flexible sentencing framework for supervising sex offenders in the community and after release from prison. They are much under-used, as we described in chapter 2, and greater use could be made of these orders and of the potential to attach specific requirements to them, especially if supervision is strengthened as recommended in this report.

2   Sentencers need to know what they can expect to follow from a sentence. Other recommendations in this report should allow them to have greater clarity about the nature and level of supervision to be provided and about the potential for more extended supervision periods for some offenders. The length of probation is frequently determined according to the seriousness of the current offence. The length of supervision should be based on the risk an offender poses following a full assessment of the risk by the SER writer.

3   If they are to have confidence in community disposals, sentencers also need information on the efficacy of sentences and the results of requirements they attach to orders. In part this can only come through further research and evaluation. Yet each sentence is an individual decision taken in the light of the unique circumstances of each case. We consider that it would be valuable to the court and salutary for the offender for there to be provision for a report back to the Court after the offender has completed his or her participation in a personal change programme to inform the Court of the outcomes. This should not require a re-appearance of the offender.

Extending monitoring and supervision

Recommendation 2

The statutory requirement to register should be extended to include offenders convicted of serious crimes where the crime had a sexual element. Legislation providing for longer

supervision (for up to ten years) of offenders following release from custody should be introduced and the effect of this should be monitored.

4   Registration is not a panacea and, drawing from the American experience, considerable effort will be required to maintain the accuracy and integrity of the systems.

5   Public confidence in the registration systems is vital; the greater this confidence the less likely are calls for community or public notification with its attendant problems. In view of this it is important that registration should apply to all serious sex offenders. One approach would be to legislate for registration requirements to be made, where judged appropriate by sentencers, in all cases where an offence clearly has a sexual element.

6   Sex offenders present a particularly difficult risk for the police and community criminal justice services to manage and the research evidence, together with the age profiles of offenders, indicates that the risks continue for many years. Intensive supervision cannot generally be maintained for prolonged periods (beyond three years). However, longer supervision arrangements tailored to the specific case and varied according to the degree of assessed risk at any one time would provide further protection for the public.

Focussing supervision on oversight and risk management

Recommendation 3

Criminal justice social work services should be planned and organised as providing a portfolio of services including supervision, advice and assistance and work with offenders on personal change. The purpose of supervision should be clearly defined as the oversight of offenders and the assessment, management and reduction of risk. Supervision plans should be based on systematic risk assessments. Local authorities and police forces should make local agreements for collaboration in risk assessment and management. The Scottish Office should consult local authorities and others on developing key aspects of the steps for strengthening supervision outlined in this report including strengthening the working links between local authorities and the Scottish Prison Service.

7   This recommendation flows from our definition of supervision as:

Planned arrangements for overseeing sex offenders in the community, designed to manage and reduce the risk posed by the offender within the framework of a statutory order which may be either a community disposal or a post-custodial requirement. The supervision plan includes an assessment of risk and how the supervisor will check on the activities and circumstances of an offender, monitor compliance with all requirements of the order (taking action where necessary) and collaborate with other agencies in managing and reducing risk.

8   Defining supervision in this way is not to imply that this also defines all the work that a supervising social worker may undertake. They should also provide advice and assistance, where that will reduce risk and promote the reintegration of the offender. They may also work with the offender to bring about personal change.

9   Risk assessment is not an exact science. Some approaches emphasise the professional or clinical judgement of the person making the assessment, while others emphasise the identification of factors that can be shown as statistically significant in predicting risk. There are no fail-safe methods and best practice will combine the insights of different disciplines and knowledge of research findings, with careful consideration of the individual offender and information about him or her.

10   Risk assessment is not easy. The literature review highlights the difficulties and our consultation has confirmed these. However, it is essential and securing greater consistency in risk assessment and the evaluation of methods should be given priority. Training and agency support for those making risk assessments is crucial.

11   The assessment should include an assessment of the likelihood of re-offending, the potential seriousness of any future offending and an assessment of what factors in the offender's social and personal circumstances need to be addressed to reduce the risk. Risk assessments should also be undertaken at key points in an offender's life such as release from prison, changes in personal circumstances or where there are concerns about behaviour.

12   There should be a clear plan for supervision based on the risk an offender poses. The overall plan of work with the offender and any plans for treatment or personal change programmes will take into account their social and personal circumstances and other work required to reduce the risk of re-offending.

13   In complex cases social workers may act as supervision case managers putting together a package of arrangements aimed at managing the risks posed by an offender.

14   Putting in place some, or all, of the steps for strengthening supervision outlined in chapter 2 needs detailed consideration and some would require additional resources.

Developing and evaluating treatment and personal change programmes

Recommendation 4

The Scottish Office should consult on whether a specialist residential facility for assessment and personal change programmes should be established and, if so, how the facility should be funded and run, taking particular account of the potential for such a unit to assist both the Scottish Prison Service and local authorities. Consideration should be given to establishing specialist provision for younger sex offenders, perhaps within one of the wings of the new secure care unit planned to replace St Mary's, Kenmure.

15   Some offenders on community sentences, such as probation, or released from prison need close supervision coupled with intensive programmes to bring about real change in their thinking and behaviour. Therefore there will continue to be a need for access to residential programmes of the kind provided by the Wolvercote Clinic in the South of England. There are real practical difficulties in placing offenders at such a distance and several submissions to the review argued that Scotland needs its own national residential facility. A small number of sex offenders from Scotland are referred to Wolvercote for assessment and some participate in the change programmes because there is no comparable facility in Scotland.

16   It is difficult to predict accurately the numbers of people who would be eligible for, and benefit from, the intensive programme provided in a residential setting. Referral to Wolvercote presently appears to depend upon the knowledge of individual probation officers and the availability of a range of other resources in local areas. If the centre admitted people whose abuse of children is established in civil proceedings or Children's Hearings, as Wolvercote does, it seems likely that there would be substantial demand for residential provision in Scotland if this were available. This may operate alongside the use of the Exclusion Order in child protection proceedings.

17   In considering the need for such a unit further, special consideration should be given to the possibility of the facility serving in some way both local authorities and the prison service. This might take the form of a community facility with intensive oversight and staffing, accepting referrals from local authorities and prisons (perhaps prisoners nearing parole). Alternatively it might be run within the prison service and accept referrals from local authorities. Various models are possible. Such a development would be unique and a number of difficulties stand in its way. However, it would strongly support the developing partnership between the prison service and community criminal justice services which we consider is vital in this field.

18   Young people's sexual offending must be more effectively addressed at an early stage if their progression to more serious offending in adulthood is to be prevented. There is an opportunity to tackle these problems during the redevelopment of St Mary's Kenmure secure unit in the West of Scotland. This unit will comprise five discrete living units within the building. One of these could be designated for young people convicted of, or under supervision for, sexual offences with programmes comparable to those in community-based and prison facilities. This will enable staff to build up a reservoir of skills and expertise and enable consistent access to change programmes for young people who need it. It cannot, in our view, be right to accommodate in the same unit boys convicted of sexual assault and children in secure accommodation for their own protection (for instance, girls held securely to prevent them harming themselves or absconding to work as prostitutes). More differentiated provision of secure care for children is therefore required.

Recommendation 5

The Scottish Office should review with local authorities the skill-mix of staff in criminal justice social work services in order to

- **increase the availability of a wider range of professional disciplines, including psychology, to support the work of qualified social workers in personal change programmes**

- **consider greater use of unqualified staff in carrying out supervision tasks allied to oversight of offenders activities whilst retaining the responsibility for supervision case management with social workers.**

This should include reviewing the arrangements for inter-authority collaboration in the provision of specialist services. So that evidence-based practice can be more rapidly developed across the country a central resource should be established providing training and consultancy in criminal justice social work services and their management.

19   Workers from other disciplines or professional backgrounds may have an important, and in some cases, unique contribution to make to the management of sex offenders in the community. Other professionals, particularly psychologists, have a central role in the assessment and management of sex offenders in hospitals and other health settings, and in prisons. The mix of different perspectives and knowledge which results from different professional groups working together can enrich the contribution of each professional group, and enhance the overall quality of work undertaken with the offender. There is also scope to use non-professional staff to undertake some elements of monitoring or of supervision (in our definition of this term), thereby freeing up qualified professional staff to undertake the more highly-skilled components which may be associated with supervision, such as the delivery of personal change programmes or other work focused on tackling offending and related problems.

20   Sex offenders represent a relatively small proportion of the people entering the criminal

justice system. Knowledge and expertise in the management of sexual offenders in the community is not, therefore, widespread amongst either practitioners or their managers.

21   Social work training provision, at both pre- and post-qualifying levels, should be adapted and developed to better equip staff to deal effectively with the assessment, supervision and management of sex offenders, and to meet the legitimate expectations of the public about the management of these cases. Whilst there are pockets of knowledge and expertise across the country, such knowledge and skills are not easily disseminated at present.

Addressing long-term issues

Recommendation 6

The Scottish Office and local authorities should consider piloting projects specifically focused on developing the relationship and parenting skills of boys and men. The projects should be targeted but draw on general education provision. All education authorities should have in place a Personal Safety programme promoting pupil's skills, knowledge and understanding to assist them in living safely and to feel empowered to reject inappropriate behaviours.

22   Sex offenders are a heterogeneous group differing widely in social class, educational achievement, social attitudes, family backgrounds and experiences. Nevertheless one factor stands out above all others. Almost all violent sexual crime and sexual abuse of children is committed by men or boys. It must be remembered, however, that whilst most sex offenders are men, very few men are sex offenders.

23   Some argue that the different experiences or attributes of men and women are a background factor. Generally girls are educated early on into looking after the needs of children, through play and socialisation. Girls are more likely than boys to help look after younger siblings or care for other people's children. The nature of child bearing strongly supports women's bonding with their children. This caring focus has been established over countless generations, but is changing. Boys' experiences are different. Generally boys will rehearse little in the way of caring in their play, and many will rehearse violence in protection of themselves, their family or society. This protective focus has been established over countless generations, but is changing.

24   Research enables us to draw some early conclusions about the kind of experiences and characteristics that result in a greater likelihood of violent and abusive behaviour (for instance, the damaging effects of early separation and the importance of fathers bonding with their children when they are very young). In part at least this may point to the importance of the development of nurturing and bonded relationships as internal controls prohibiting abusive acts and treating others as objects.

25   Many of the most entrenched offenders have experienced sexual or physical, and emotional abuse within their own families. Often they have had no positive models of parenting which demonstrate relationships founded on mutual respect and caring, or how to love and care for a child of their own. Many of these offenders have been looked after by local Councils in local authority accommodation throughout their adolescence and development into young adults. They have little opportunity to develop relationship skills or their own parenting abilities. Their relationships with their carers may be transitory and instrumental rather than expressive.

26   Many young people looked after by local authorities grow up as confident and highly competent people. Others find that they are woefully ill-equipped for relationships in

general and particularly for the demanding relationships involved in being a parent. Young people who have been looked after by a local authority are by no means the only group at risk in this way. The consequences can be tragic. Local authorities are well placed to develop pilot schemes (possibly run by voluntary organisations) to educate adolescent boys whom they deem to be at risk of not developing good parenting skills, to better equip them for their caring roles as partners and as fathers.

27   More broadly, education for men and boys outside school should be made available through community education facilities for those whose circumstances make them particularly vulnerable or for whom mainstream education is unlikely to be effective in promoting positive messages about their role in caring for others. Courses on fathering might be promoted in colleges of further education and within adult education courses. Current limited provision in prisons might be extended. As sex offenders come from all classes of society, private sector schools will wish to consider the applicability of these matters in their circumstances.

28   This report concentrates on steps to reduce the likelihood of convicted offenders re-offending, but it is also important that children and young people are aware of their rights and of how to keep themselves safe. Some authorities have excellent programmes in place; the quality and spread of the Edinburgh council's "Feeling Yes, Feeling No" programme is a good example. In other authorities the provision is patchy. Several authorities have run Personal Safety programmes for several years and, with parental partnership and professional inter-disciplinary co-operation, these have been greatly appreciated and deemed to be very worthwhile. These programmes should be available to all children in Scotland wherever they live and whether they attend a local authority or independent school.

The need for national oversight

Recommendation 7

Ministers should consider the appointment, for three years, of an Expert Panel on Sex Offending to assist the strategic collaboration of local authorities, the prison service, police, health and voluntary organisations involved in dealing with sex offending. The Panel's prime remit should be to take forward the recommendations of this report and the strengthening of services contingent on them.

The Panel should end three years after its first meeting unless Ministers determine otherwise.

29   We consider that, for a time, some form of high-level co-ordinating body to oversee all work with sex offenders in Scotland would provide a useful mechanism for taking forward these recommendations for ensuring effective strategic collaboration between agencies to strengthen services in the ways set out in his report. In general this work stands to be undertaken by The Scottish Office but a highly focused group set up for a limited period would assist agencies in establishing a new approach in this field and promote consistency across the country.

30   Good strategic collaboration is essential to get maximum benefit from new initiatives. For example, successful implementation of the Sex Offenders Act 1997 depends on co-ordination across Scotland, especially between the police and social work services, and consistency in pursuit of shared objectives. Local collaboration is often excellent, but not always, and is not made easier by the fact that in many areas the police, local authority and health board boundaries are different.

31   All the agencies involved already have extensive planning systems and for this reason we have rejected calls for further local planning requirements specifically about sex offending. However, we do consider that some central lead must be given to co-ordination and local planning if reasonable consistency is to be achieved. Consistency is important in this field; having different policies on accommodation or monitoring or supervision in different areas would rapidly undermine the effectiveness of services.

32   The Panel should include representation from local authorities, police, courts, prisons, health services and voluntary bodies. The Convenor would be appointed by Ministers. The Scottish Office should provide administrative and professional support. In addition to the functions listed above, the Panel would act as a reference point for new issues.

33   One of the key messages of the review is that dealing effectively with sex offenders depends on the ability to manage information. A Scottish Panel on Sex Offending could promote excellence in the management of information about sex offenders in each of the different ways that it is needed to reduce sex offending. These are:

- managing information about individuals convicted of sex offences to promote public protection;

- managing information between and within organisations to ensure that those who need to have information have it, and those who do not, do not;

- managing information about the outcomes of sentences and of work with sex offenders to improve supervision, treatment and personal change programmes and to inform sentencing; and,

- managing information from research about sex offenders and sex offending to inform the work of professionals in practice and to enhance the assessment of risk.

34   Knowledge about sex offending is uncertain and risk assessment, personal change programmes and treatment for sex offenders remain at an early stage of development. If all agencies follow guidelines on risk assessment based on the most up-to-date knowledge co-ordinated by a Scottish Panel on Sex Offending, the Courts and the public can have greater confidence in how risk is assessed and how the agencies work together in managing and reducing risk. Risk assessment will also develop more effectively. Treatment and personal change programmes will develop better and retain greater confidence if they consistently meet certain basic requirements both in the basis for their provision and for their evaluation.

35   To do this the Panel will need to establish mechanisms for reviewing research and statistical information and considering the implications for Scottish policy and practice.

Acknowledgements

In undertaking this review we spoke with staff from a number of local authorities and other agencies. All were helpful and many have made significant contributions to the review. Given the sensitive nature of the review not everyone wished to be named and so we are listing the organisations rather than the individuals who work in them. In all we received help from over 70 people from the agencies listed below.

Aberdeenshire Council
Albrae Project
Angus Council
Argyll and Bute Council
Association of Chief Officers of Probation
Association of Chief Police Officers in Scotland
Barnardo's - The Bridge Project
Central Constabulary
City of Edinburgh Council
Derwent Initiative, Newcastle
Dumbarton Project
Dundee Council
Durham Constabulary
Durham Probation Service
East Dunbartonshire Council
Falkirk Council
ISSO Project
Lennox Castle Hospital (Forensic Service)
New Scotland Yard, Paedophilia Unit
Northumbria Probation Service Sex offender Unit
NOTA, Scottish Section
Perth and Kinross Council
Peterhead Prison
Polmont Prison
SACRO
Scottish Children's Reporter Administration
Scottish Prison Service
The State Hospital
Stirling Council
The Tay Project
Tayside Police Force
West Yorks Probation Service
The Wolvercote Clinic, Surrey

We also spoke with several sex offenders.

Survey Responses

All 32 local authorities responded to the survey of community-based programmes for sex offenders. The survey was adapted from a questionnaire used by the ACOP (Association of Chief Officers of Probation) with their permission.

Acknowledgements

Consultation Returns

Aberdeen City Council, Social Work Dept
Aberdeenshire Council, Social Work
Angus Council, Social Work
Argyle and Clyde Health Board
Argyll & Bute Council, Corporate Services
Association of Chief Police Officers in Scotland
Association of Directors of Social Work
Ayrshire and Arran Health Board
British Association of Early Childhood Education (Aberdeen Branch)
British Medical Association: Scottish Office
British Psychological Society
Capability Scotland
Central Scotland Healthcare
Centre for Residential Child Care, The
Chartered Institute of Housing in Scotland
Childline Scotland
Church of Scotland, Board of Social Responsibility, The
City of Edinburgh Council, The
Clackmannanshire Council, Housing and Social Services
Dumfries & Galloway Council, Social Work
Dumfries & Galloway Health Board
Dumfries and Galloway Community Health, Crichton Royal Hospital
Dundee City Council, Social Work
East Ayrshire Council, Social Work
East Dunbartonshire Council, Social Work
East Lothian Children's Panel
East Lothian Council, Social Work
East Renfrewshire Council, Social Work
Falkirk Council, Education Service
Falkirk Council, Social Work Services
Fife Council, Education Service
Fife Council, Social Work Service
Fife Health Board
General Teaching Council for Scotland
Glasgow City Council, Social Work
Highland Council, The
Inverclyde Council, Social & Community Division
Lanarkshire Healthcare NHS Trust
Law Society of Scotland, The
Lennox Castle Hospital
Lothian Health Board
Mental Welfare Commission for Scotland
Midlothian Council, Social Services
Moray Council, Social Work
National Society for the Prevention of Cruelty to Children, The
NCH Action for Children Scotland
North Ayrshire Council, Housing Services
North Ayrshire Council, Social Work
North Lanarkshire Council
Orkney Islands Council

Perth & Kinross Council
Perth & Kinross Healthcare, Murray Royal Hospital
Renfrewshire Council
Renfrewshire Healthcare NHS Trust
Royal College of Nursing
Royal College of Psychiatrists: The Scottish Division
Royal Hospital for Sick Children
SACRO
Save the Children Fund (Scotland)
Scottish Association of Children's Panels, The
Scottish Children's Reporter Administration
Scottish Council for Civil Liberties
Scottish Council for Independent Schools
Scottish Council for Single Homeless
Scottish Homes
Scottish Prison Service
Scottish Secondary Teachers' Association
SENSE (Scotland)
Sheriff Principals
Shetlands Islands Council, Social Work Department
South Ayrshire Council, Community Services
South Lanarkshire Council
St Joseph's, Rosewell
Stirling Council, Housing and Social Services
Volunteer Development Scotland
West Dunbartonshire Council, Education
West Dunbartonshire Council, Social Work & Housing
West Lothian Council, Social Work
Womens National Commission
Womens Royal Voluntary Service
YMCA Scotland

Appendix 1: What Does Research Tell Us?

Introduction

1   This paper is based on a review of research literature about sex offenders and their behaviour. Its purpose was to identify the research contribution to our understanding of: the nature and extent of sex offending; the characteristics of the people involved; the explanations for their behaviour; and the ways in which they can be dealt with effectively. It was prepared by the Central Research Unit for the review of arrangements for the supervision of sex offenders in the community in Scotland.

2   The review focuses primarily on studies from 1980 onwards but includes earlier relevant research where it has been identified. The literature reviewed includes both quantitative and qualitative research studies, recent analyses of such studies and comparisons of findings from different research accounts. The paper has 6 sections and these highlight research knowledge about key aspects of sex offending. These are:

Section 1:   The nature of sex offences

Section 2:   The extent of sex offending

Section 3:   Characteristics of sex offenders

Section 4:   Theories about why people commit sex offences

Section 5:   Dealing with sex offenders

Section 6:   Summary of key issues highlighted in the research

The Nature Of Sex offences

3   A very broad range of behaviours can be classified as sex offences. These include rape, sexual assault, indecent exposure, possession of pornographic material and consensual sexual acts that are illegal, including prostitution offences. There are some differences in the literature about what are considered to be sex offences; for example, some writers, who attach importance to the imbalance of power which often exists in social relations, argue that serial murderers of women or children should be viewed as sex offenders, whether or not they sexually assault their victims[1]. Most of the research literature, however, focuses on offences involving behaviour of a sexual nature which does not necessarily include physical contact but which is non-consensual.

4   Consent is widely discussed in the literature since this is a major issue in identifying sex offences[2]. Most sex offences are perpetrated in private and in many cases attempts to prove that an offence took place depend on determining whether or not the victim consented to the act. In the case of sex offences against children the issue of consent is less problematic:

---

[1] Sampson, A (1994) *Acts of Abuse: Sex Offenders in the Criminal Justice System*, London: Routledge.

[2] See, for example, Doyle, C (1994) *Child Sexual Abuse: A Guide for Health Professionals*, London: Chapman and Hall.

children under the age of 16 cannot consent to sexual acts as they lack the legal capacity to do so in Scots law. Nevertheless, issues of consent arise in cases of sex offences against children where both perpetrator and victim lack legal capacity. Similarly, consent is at issue where those involved, whether as perpetrators or victims, have learning difficulties. In all cases, determining whether or not consent was given involves consideration of whether force or coercion was used to gain the victim's compliance.

5   Questions of force and coercion are fundamental in the identification of sex offending. Research indicates that sex offences are perpetrated primarily by men[3] against women and children. The nature of relationships between the sexes, and between adults and children, are therefore of prime importance in this area of offending. Research which discusses this issue directly highlights the need to understand the imbalance in relations of power and dependency which exists in some settings[4]. This is an important element of the context in which sex offences are often perpetrated. For example, sex offences are often committed by perpetrators who are in positions of trust in relation to their victims[5]. This is particularly so in the case of sexual abuse of children by adults, where fathers, stepfathers and other carers are the main perpetrators of such offences[6]. Identifying sex offences against this background is further compounded by difficulties in recording and prosecuting such offences.

The Extent Of Sex Offending

6   Most studies of sex offences include attempts to describe the extent of sex offending and there is a substantial literature on measuring incidence and prevalence. Incidence is a measure of the number of such offences committed; prevalence is usually a measure of the proportion of victims of sex offending in the population. Most of the work on prevalence was undertaken in North America during the 1970s and 1980s, although there are prevalence studies from other countries. Studies of incidence are more routinely undertaken and many are based on published official crime statistics. There is, however, consensus in the literature that official statistics under-record the incidence of sex offending.

Incidence

7   Scottish Office statistics on criminal justice provide information about the number of recorded sex offences and the number of people convicted of a sex offence each year. Details about those statistics and the definitions used in collecting data about sex offences committed in Scotland are contained in the annex at the end of this paper. There are 3 main difficulties with using these statistics to describe the extent of sex offending:

- only information on recorded sex offences and convicted sex offenders are included;
- convictions may be for lesser charges than the original charge;
- not all offences with a sexual content are prosecuted as such, for example some may be prosecuted as breach of the peace.

8   Research suggests that many sex offences are not reported because victims feel unable

---

[3] Women also commit sex offences but research suggests that very few sex offenders are female.
[4] See, for example, Brown, H and Turk, V (1992) *Defining Sexual Abuse as it affects Adults with Learning Disabilities*, Mental Handicap Vol 20, June.
[5] Lloyd, C & Walmsley, R (1989) *Changes in Rape Offences and Sentencing*, Home Office Research Study No. 105, London: HMSO.
[6] Finkelhor, D and Associates (1986) *A Sourcebook on Child Sexual Abuse*, London: Sage.

to cope with the consequences associated with reporting. It also suggests that the number of convictions do not reflect the extent of offending due to the difficulties associated with obtaining evidence for successful prosecution. Studies deal with these difficulties by using information from a variety of sources to estimate incidence and prevalence. Such information includes other official statistics, for example police clear up rates, crime surveys and other research involving self-reports by victims and offenders. Studies which have drawn on offenders' self reports to estimate incidence of sex offences have found that sex offenders admit to more crimes than those for which they are convicted[7].

Prevalence

9   Nearly all of the prevalence studies of sex offending focus on child sexual abuse and gather information about experience as victims of such abuse from adult populations. The definition of sexual abuse varies between studies, with some using a broad definition including non contact acts, some including contact of an explicitly sexual nature, and others using a narrow definition including only genital contact. Similarly, studies vary in their definition of 'child', with some measuring abuse before puberty, some before age 15 and others including abuse suffered up to 16 or 17 years old. Studies also use different definitions of perpetrators, with some research only including abusive acts perpetrated by adults. Such differences contribute to the variations in prevalence rates found by studies.

10   A comparative study of international prevalence rates for child sexual abuse found that rates ranged from 7% to 36% of the female population and 3% to 29% for men across the 21 countries included[8]. No studies of prevalence have been undertaken in Scotland; however, a British study[9] undertaken in the early 1980s found that just over 10% of a random sample of 2,019 adult men and women had suffered some type of (broadly defined) child sexual abuse by the age of 16: the rate for females was 12% and the rate for males 8%. A review[10] of prevalence rates of child sex abuse among female populations in 10 North American studies between 1975 and 1985 showed that these rates ranged from 6% to 62%. One of these studies[11], which used a narrow contact definition found that 28% of a random sample of 930 women had been sexually abused before the age of 14. This percentage rose to 38% when abuse up to the age of 18 was included. Variation in prevalence rates identified by studies highlights the sensitivity of figures to different definitions and measures of sex offending. This underlines the need for caution in counting sex offenders.

Recidivism rates for sex offenders

11   Recidivism studies attempt to measure the incidence of reoffending by convicted offenders. Reconviction is generally used as a proxy for reoffending, although some studies

---

[7] Abel, G C, Becker, J V, Mittleman, M S, Cunningham-Rathner, J, Rouleau, J L and Murphy, W D (1987) *Self Reported Crimes of Non-incarcerated Paraphiliacs*, Journal of Interpersonal Violence Vol. 2, No. 6, pp 3-25. Groth, M A, Longo, R E, McFadin, J B (1982) *Undetected Recidivism Among Rapists and Child Molesters*, cited in Weinrott, M R and Saylor, M (1991) Self Report of Crimes Committed by Sex Offenders, Journal of Interpersonal Violence 6, 3.

[8] Finkelhor, D (1994) *The International Epidemiology of Child Sexual Abuse*, Child Abuse and Neglect, Vol. 18, No. 5, pp 409-417.

[9] Baker, A and Duncan, S (1985) *Child Sexual Abuse: A Study of Prevalence in Great Britain*, Child Abuse and Neglect 15:9.

[10] Peters, S D, Wyatt, G E and Finkelhor, D (1986) Prevalence, in Finkelhor, D and Associates (eds) *A Sourcebook on Child Sexual Abuse*, London: Sage.

[11] Russell, Diana (1984) *Sexual Exploitation: Rape, Child Sexual Abuse, Sexual Harassment*, Newbury Park: Sage.

are based on rearrest for further offences. Recidivism figures may indicate either reconviction for any type of offending or may relate only to offences which are the same as for the original conviction. Studies to identify recidivism rates for sex offenders face the same difficulties of identification and recording as other studies of sex offending. These are: under-reporting, delayed reporting, and low levels of prosecution. In addition, lengthy investigation and prosecution procedures can contribute to delay in recording convictions for reoffending. Studies[12] to identify indicators of risk of reconviction among offenders have found that prior conviction, not necessarily for the same offence, is an indicator of a high risk of reconviction. This is also true for sex offenders.

12   Two major national[13] studies which identify recidivism rates for different types of offenders have been undertaken, one by the Home Office in England and Wales[14] based on reconviction rates, the other by the US Justice Department[15] based on rearrest rates. Both studies found low recidivism rates for sex offenders relative to other offenders. The Home Office study found that in a 2-year follow-up period sex offenders had the lowest general reconviction rates of all offenders: 25% of sex offenders were reconvicted after 2 years, though 15% of these were for further sex offences. This contrasts with the 47% of offenders committing violent crimes who were reconvicted after 2 years, though of these 27% were reconvicted of further crimes of violence. The US study found that in a 3-year follow-up period general recidivism rates for rapists were 52% and for sexual assaulters 48%. These were among the lowest general rates, although murderers and those convicted of negligent manslaughter had lower rearrest rates: 43% and 42% respectively. The American study found that sex offenders had the lowest rearrest rates for further offences of the same type apart from murderers: 25% of sexual offenders were rearrested for subsequent sex offences; 7% of murderers were rearrested for murder.

13   A further study[16] looked only at recidivism rates for sex offenders and was based on 61 data sets from 6 countries. The authors found, after an average 4 to 5 year follow up period, average recidivism rates for sex offenders are: 13.4% for sex offences; 12.2% for non-sexual violent offences; and 36.3% for any offences. Rapists were found to be much more likely to commit non-sexual violent offences than child molesters. High levels of sexual deviance and, to a lesser extent, a history of prior sex offences, in particular against unrelated and unknown victims, and against male victims, were found to be the strongest predictors of the likelihood of reoffending sexually.

14   Research on recidivism is often based on following offenders for 2 years or less. Factors contributing to difficulties in identifying sex offences (see paragraph 9) will affect identified recidivism rates for this group of offenders and this implies that recidivism studies of sex offenders need to have longer follow-up periods. While only a few studies have looked at reconviction over longer periods, findings from these studies show that:

- some sex offenders are not re-convicted for the first time until over twenty years after completing a prison sentence for an offence[17];

---

[12] Lloyd, C, Mair, G and Hough, M (1994) *Explaining Reconviction Rates: A critical analysis*, London: HMSO, and Thornton D & Travers R (1991) 'A Longtitudinal study of the criminal behaviour of convicted sex offenders' Paper delivered to Prison Service Psychlogy Conference, Scarborough 16-18th October.

[13] There may be other national studies of recidivism among convicted offenders, particularly non-English language studies, but none were found in the literature searched.

[14] Lloyd, C, Mair, G and Hough, M (1994) *Explaining Reconviction Rates: A critical analysis*, London: HMSO.

[15] Beck, A J and Shipley, B E (1989) *Recidivism of Prisoners Released in 1983*, Washington: US Department of Justice.

[16] Hanson, R K, & Bussiere, M T (1996) *Predictors of Sexual Offender Recidivism: A meta-analysis*, Public Works and Services of Canada.

[17] Barker, M and Morgan, R (1993) *Sex Offenders: a framework for the evaluation of community-based treatment*, London: Home Office.

- recidivism rates for sexual offences have been found to double, from 11% when measured between 0 and 5 years after release to 22% when measured between 5 and 22 years after release[18].

15   It is recognised in the literature that recidivism studies of sex offenders need longer follow-ups than for other groups of offenders. For example, the Home Office researchers who carried out the national study cited above recommended follow-up periods of at least 5 years for sex offenders. An ongoing Home Office evaluation[19] of sex offender programmes has measured recidivism after a 2-year follow-up period and will measure recidivism again 5 and 10 years after programme completion.

16   Most recidivism rates are based on studies involving small numbers of offenders and studies use different measures to calculate recidivism, i.e. reconviction, rearrest or further charges. Although the recidivism rates for sex offenders identified in the literature vary, there is general consensus in the literature that recidivism rates differ between different types of sex offenders. A study by Marshall and Barbaree[20] found that:

- exhibitionists have the highest rate of recidivism, ranging between 41% and 71%;

- recidivism rates for non-familial child sex abusers range between 10% and 40%;

- recidivism rates for rapists range between 7% and 35%;

- familial child sex abusers have the lowest recidivism rates, ranging from 4% to 10%.

17   Other studies of recidivism which looked at the age and gender of the victim suggest that recidivism rates also differ by victim group. Findings include:

- child molesters with male victims have the highest recidivism rates, 35% compared to 18% for those with female victims[21];

- recidivism rates for non-familial sex offenders against boys range between 13% and 40%[22];

- offenders with unrelated female victims have lower reconviction rates (between 6% and 29%) than offenders with male victims[23].

18   Studies of recidivism that explicitly include analyses of additional data from police and child protection files, estimate actual reoffending rates at more than twice those calculated using reconviction data sources[24]. Difficulties in identifying the extent of sex offences place important limits on knowledge of sex offending; however, as well as providing information about the extent of sex offences, research can help by contributing information about the characteristics of offenders.

---

[18] Fisher, D (1994) Sex Offenders: Who are they? Why are they?, in Morrison, T, Erooga, M and Beckett, R (eds) *Sexual Offenders Against Children: Assessment and Treatment of Male Abusers*, London: Routledge.
[19] Hedderman, C, and Sugg, D (1996) *Does Treating Sex Offenders Reduce Sex Offending?*, Home Office Research and Statistics Directorate, Research Findings No. 45, October 1996.
[20] Marshall, W L and Barbaree, H E (1990) Outcome of Cognitive Behavioral Treatment, in Marshall, W L, Laws D R and Barbaree H E (eds), *Handbook of Sexual Assault*, New York: Plenum.
[21] Quinsey, V L, La Lumiere, M, Rice, M and Harris, G (1995) Predicting Sexual Offences in Campbell, J C (ed) *Assessing Dangerousness: violence by sexual offenders, batterers and child abusers*, London: Sage.
[22] Fisher, D (1994) Sex Offenders: Who are they? Why are they?, in Morrison, T, Erooga, M, and Beckett, R (eds) *Sexual Offenders Against Children: Assessment and Treatment of Male Abusers*, London: Routledge.
[23] Quinsey, V L, Rice, M and Harris, G (1995) *Actuarial Prediction of Sexual Recidivism*, in Journal of Interpersonal Violence, Vol. 10, No. 1, pp 85-105, March 1995.
[24] Marshall, W L, Jones, R, Ward, T, Johnston, P and Barbaree, H E (1991) *Treatment Outcome with Sex Offenders*, Clinical Psychology Review, Vol 11, pp 465-485.

Characteristics Of Sex Offenders

19   The literature makes it very clear that the nature of sex offending is diverse and that there is a range of types of offender within this distinct group. Statements about the nature of sex offending depend on our knowledge and analysis of known offences and offenders, who may differ from offenders who are never caught. Because it appears that much sex offending may be hidden from view, this is important. Studies of the characteristics of sex offenders often collect information about sex offenders from psychological profiles and from the accounts of victims. Much of the information available about the nature of sex offending comes from sex offenders themselves. Some writers view this as problematic because this group of offenders are widely perceived as prone to deny their offences and to minimise the extent and impact of their offences. Nevertheless, findings from some self-report studies (see paragraph 8) are that sex offenders admit to more offences than those for which they are convicted.

20   Within the research literature, sex offenders have been distinguished in a number of ways:

- by the characteristics of perpetrators;
- by the characteristics of their victims;
- by the relationship between perpetrator and victim; and
- by the nature of the offending behaviour.

21   Within these categories further distinctions are often made. In particular, sex offenders who abuse children are often subdivided into those who are related to the children they abuse; those who abuse children to whom they are not related but with whom they have some relationship of trust; and those who abuse children who are strangers to them. A further distinction is sometimes made between those whose abuse involves physical contact and those whose abuse does not. Levels of violence used in perpetrating the offence are also used to distinguish types of sex offenders.

22   There is consensus in studies of populations which are not exclusively sex offenders that sex offenders do not differ significantly from general populations when measured on variables such as level of intelligence, age, ethnicity, education, psychiatric status, and arousal to deviant images.

23   Studies which focus on sex offenders agree on the following points[25].

- Almost all sex offenders are male and perpetrators include both juveniles and adults.
- Sex offenders come from all socio-economic groups though there are higher prosecution rates among lower socio-economic groups.
- The majority of sex offenders are not mentally ill, in the sense of having a diagnosable, psychiatric illness. However, some sex offenders have learning difficulties.
- The majority of sex offenders can be classified by clinicians either as individuals with anti-social personalities or as paraphiliacs[26].

---

[25] See, for example, Barker, M and Morgan, R (1993) *Sex Offenders: a framework for the evaluation of community-based treatment*, London: Home Office.

[26] A paraphilia is 'arousal in response to sexual objects or situations that are not part of normative arousal activity patterns and whose essential features are intense sexual urges and sexually arousing fantasies generally involving non-human objects, the suffering or humiliation of one's self or one's partner, or children or other non-consenting persons.' (American Psychiatric Association (1987) Diagnostic and Statistical Manual of Mental Disorders 3rd edition (revised) APA)

24   Most of the evidence about sex offenders is about men who sexually abuse children. There is also some evidence about the characteristics of other types of sex offenders, in particular about rapists and indecent exposers. There is less evidence about sex offenders who are juveniles and there is very little evidence about the characteristics of female sex offenders and about sex offenders who have learning difficulties. The literature is largely silent on the characteristics of sex offenders in relation to pornography and obscenity offences. Information about those who are convicted rapists, child sex abusers and indecent exposers is summarised in the following sections. These findings are drawn from a number of studies, and we have relied heavily on Barker and Morgan's review of research results and Waterhouse et al's Scottish study, which included in-depth interviews with the most serious sex offenders against children in Scotland and which provides valuable qualitative evidence about this group of offenders.

Rapists

25   This group is characterised both by the serious nature of the offence and the age of the victim. Those convicted of rape or sexual assault against adults are included in this category. Research findings about this group include the following:

- rapists tend to be younger than child sex abusers[27];

- most rapes are not perpetrated by strangers but by men known intimately to the victim or by men who are acquaintances[28];

- compared to child molesters, rapists are perceived to commit fewer offences and are less likely to report arousal to deviant sexual behaviour[29];

- rapists have been found to score at levels similar to non sex offenders in tests measuring deviant sexual arousal[30].

Indecent exposers

26   Indecent exposure is one of the most common sex offences. Research findings about exhibitionists are that:

- offences tend to be committed as part of compulsive and repetitive behaviour patterns[31];

- convicted indecent exposers tend to be older on average than other types of sex offenders[32];

---

[27] Barker, M and Morgan, R (1993) *Sex Offenders: a framework for the evaluation of community-based treatment*, London: Home Office.
[28] Lloyd, C & Walmsley, R (1989) *Changes in Rape Offences and Sentencing*, Home Office Research Study No. 105, London: HMSO.
[29] Abel, G C and Rouleau, J L (1990) The Nature and Extent of Sexual Assault, in Marshall W L, Laws, D R and Barbaree H E (eds) *Handbook of Sexual Assault*, pp 9-20, New York: Plenum.
[30] Barbaree, H E (1990) Stimulus Control of Sexual Arousal: its role in sexual assault, in Marshall, W L, Laws, D R and Barbaree, H E (eds) *Handbook of Sexual Assault*, pp 115-138, New York: Plenum.
[31] Daniel, C J (1987) Shame aversion therapy and social skills training with an indecent exposer, in McGurk, B J, Thornton, D M and Williams, M (eds) *Applying Psychology to Imprisonment: Theory and Practice*, pp 247-254, London: HMSO.
[32] West, D (1987) *Sexual Crimes and Confrontations*, Cambridge Studies in Criminology, Aldershot: Gower.

- indecent exposure may sometimes be either a precursor to further acts or lead in the longer term to other sex offences[33].

Child sexual abusers

27   Sex offenders who abuse children are the most studied group in the research literature. Studies of these offenders generally distinguish 2 types of child sex abusers: familial child sex abusers and non-familial child sex abusers.

Familial child sex abusers

28   Findings about familial child sex abusers are:

- most familial child sex abusers live in the home of the victim at the time of the offence[34];
- familial child sex abusers are more likely to offend against female children[35];
- familial child sex abusers tend to have fewer victims (but may commit more offences) than non-familial child sex abusers[36];
- many familial child sex abusers do not show deviant sexual arousal to child stimuli[37];
- many familial child sex abusers appear passive, dependent and isolated individuals, with no masculine identification[38];

Non-familial child sex abusers

29   Waterhouse and her colleagues found that the non-familial child sex abusers they interviewed were more likely to have grown up in disrupted families in which they experienced significant violence from their parents and experienced periods of separation from their parents, or to have grown up in an institutional context. They were also more likely to:

- have experienced sexual abuse as a child themselves;
- have lived alone at the time of the offence;
- have previous criminal records;
- have used physical force in the offence;
- be socially inadequate;
- have been sexually attracted to young children from an early age;

---

[33] Abel, G C and Rouleau, J L (1990) The Nature and Extent of Sexual Assault, in Marshall, W L, Laws, D R and Barbaree, H E (eds) *Handbook of Sexual Assault*, pp 9-20, New York: Plenum; and Holmes, R M (1991) *Sex Crimes*, California: Sage.

[34] Waterhouse, L, Dobash, R and Carnie, J (1994) *Child Sexual Abusers*, The Scottish Office Central Research Unit: Edinburgh.

[35] Waterhouse, L, Dobash, R and Carnie, J (1994) *Child Sexual Abusers*, The Scottish Office Central Research Unit: Edinburgh.

[36] Abel, G C and Rouleau, J L (1990) The Nature and Extent of Sexual Assault, in Marshall W L, Laws, D R and Barbaree, H E (eds) *Handbook of Sexual Assault*, pp 9-20, New York: Plenum.

[37] Barker, M and Morgan, R (1993) *Sex Offenders: a framework for the evaluation of community-based treatment*, London: Home Office.

[38] Williams, L M, and Finkelhor, D (1991) Characteristics of Incestuous Fathers, in Marshall, W L, Laws, D R and Barbaree, H E (eds) *Handbook of Sexual Assault*, New York: Plenum.

⦾ commit acts of sexual violence against children while under the influence of alcohol or through loss of control in the course of sex offending.

30   These findings are consistent with those of other studies of child sex offenders. Other research findings are that non-familial child sex abusers are:

⦾ typically unassertive and socially inhibited men from authoritarian families and who had poor relationships with their parents[39];

⦾ more likely to find child pornography sexually arousing than any other types of sex offender and to have significantly different arousal patterns than non sex offenders[40];

⦾ more likely than other types of sex offender to have difficulty in controlling their sexual drives[41].

31   In addition, non-familial child sex abusers who offend against boys are portrayed in the literature as having the most entrenched deviant sexual behaviour and as having the highest rates of offending and recidivism of all child sex offenders whose abuse involves physical contact with their victim[42].

Paedophiles

32   Most child sex offenders are not paedophiles as they do not describe themselves as sexually attracted to children. However, some sex offenders are paedophiles; that is, they have a sexual orientation towards children. They form a group of people whose morality runs counter to prevailing social mores that sexual relationships involving children are wrong. Waterhouse and her colleagues divide paedophiles into three sub-groups: professional; committed; and latent. Professional paedophiles are characterised by their sexual abuse of children for financial reward, either through the making or distribution of child pornography or by procuring children for others for sexual purposes. Committed paedophiles openly admit their sexual attraction to children. This group engage in sexual activities with children for personal pleasure rather than financial reward. Latent paedophiles do not see themselves as fully sexually oriented to children and have been disturbed by their tendencies in this direction.

Other groups of sex offenders

33   There are few studies of sex offenders who are juveniles, or who have learning difficulties, or who are females. Existing research findings about juvenile sex offenders are that they do not appear to differ significantly from non-sex offenders in this age range. However, adolescent sex offenders are likely to have social skill deficits and educational difficulties[43]. It has been estimated that juveniles form a substantial proportion of all known

[39] Howard League (1985) *Unlawful Sex: offences, victims and offenders in the Criminal Justice System of England and Wales*, London: Waterlow.
[40] Murphy, W D, Haynes, M R and Worley, P J (1991) Assessment of Adult Sexual Interest, in Hollin, C R and Howells, K (eds) *Clinical Approaches to Sex Offenders and their victims*, pp 77-92, Chichester: John Wiley and Sons Ltd.
[41] Thornton, P (1992) *A framework for the assessment of sex offenders*, paper presented at 3rd European conference on Psychology and the Law, Oxford.
[42] Barker, M and Morgan, R (1993) *Sex Offenders: a framework for the evaluation of community-based treatment*, London: Home Office.
[43] O'Callaghan, D and Print, B (1994) Adolescent Sexual Abusers: research, assessment and treatment, in Morrison, T, Erooga, M and Beckett, R (eds) *Sexual Offenders Against children: practice, management and policy*, London: Routledge.

sex offenders: one study[44] found that nearly one fifth of all sex offenders in England and Wales were aged under 18. Very few studies specifically refer to sex offenders who have learning difficulties although a recent study[45] concluded that men with learning difficulties are over-represented among those who commit sex offences. Similarly, women who commit sexual offences remain a little studied group, although Fisher notes that a few studies have found that women who abuse have often been coerced into committing sex offences[46].

34   While studies which focus on sex offenders have identified that they have particular characteristics, studies of wider populations have not confirmed that these characteristics are specific to sex offenders. This means that the literature does not provide a clear indication of how to identify offenders and the level of risk that they pose. Nevertheless, there is a need to respond to sex offending and the literature highlights the theories which help to understand sex offending behaviour, and the impact of the programmes which are based on these.

Theories Of Sex Offending

35   Knowledge about the characteristics of different kinds of sex offenders is linked to theories about the attitudes and behaviour involved in sex offending. Theories of sex offending can be based on one or more factors. Originally, explanations of sex offending were based on single factors. More recently multi-factor or integrated theories have been developed from these.

Single factor theories

36   There are 3 main single factor theories of sex offending, each of which has been developed from a different perspective: organic or biological; developmental or psychological; and structural or sociological.

- Organic, or biological, theories focus on physical differences between sex offenders and others in the population, for example, in brain abnormalities and differences in hormonal levels among offenders.

- Developmental theories rely upon psychoanalytical and conditioning explanations for sex offending. According to these theories, sexual deviancy in adulthood is related to problems of psychological development in childhood. Developmental, or psychological, theories explain sex offending as a problem of the individual and therefore imply that abusive behaviour can be changed.

- Structural theories place sex offending within a wider social context and stress societal factors in explaining sex offending behaviour.

37   It is generally accepted that a single factor theory is insufficient to explain sex offending, and a number of approaches which combine some elements and insights from all three types of theory are documented in the research literature.

---

[44] Mapp, S (1996) 'Growing Pains', Community Care, p 10, 28/3/96.
[45] Day, K (1994) *Male Mentally Handicapped Sex Offenders*, British Journal of Psychiatry, 165, pp 630-639.
[46] Fisher, D (1994) Sex Offenders: Who are they? Why are they? in Morrison, T, Erooga, M, and Beckett, R (eds) *Sexual Offenders Against Children: practice, management and policy*, London: Routledge.

Integrated theories

38 Four principal integrated or multi-factoral theorists are cited in the literature: Marshall and Barbaree[47]; Wolf[48]; Finkelhor[49]; and Prentky[50]. The theories developed by these writers are based on their experience and studies of sex offenders in clinical settings in North America. The explanations offered by their theories form the basis for much of the work undertaken with sex offenders in the UK. The theories explain both the development of sex offending behaviour and the processes involved in offenders' perpetration of offences.

39 Marshall and Barbaree's integrated theory uses developmental or learning theories to explain sex offending. They maintain that sex offending occurs where an individual has failed to understand sexual norms, has not learned to control natural sexual impulses and tends to confuse sex and aggression. A combination of these factors and the opportunity to offend when the offender is feeling stressed or angry is likely to result in an offence.

40 Wolf's developmental theory claims that an individual's early history leads to the development of a certain type of personality which predisposes them towards developing deviant sexual interests. Characteristics of this type of personality include:

- egocentricity;
- poor self image;
- defensiveness;
- distorted thinking;
- obsessive thoughts and behaviour;
- social alienation; and
- sexual preoccupation.

It is also likely that the offender will have been exposed to abusive attitudes or behaviour whilst growing up.

41 Wolf's approach includes the concept of a cycle of abuse, known as the 'sexual assault cycle', to explain the relationships between the causal factors. The cycle of abuse (see Figure 1 below) begins with the individual having a poor self image, expecting rejection, withdrawing and becoming unassertive. From this withdrawn, isolated state the individual escapes through sexual fantasies and may begin to plan an offence. Following the offence the offender goes through a period of guilt which may be reduced through distorted thinking, for example blaming the victim. However, the guilt will reinforce the low self-esteem which began the cycle. The cycle itself reinforces behaviour and sex offending becomes compulsive and addictive.

---

[47] Marshall, W and Barbaree, H E (1990) An Integrated Theory of the Etiology of Sexual Offending, in Marshall, W L, Laws, D R and Barbaree, H E (eds) A Handbook of Sexual Assault, *New York: Plenum.*
[48] Wolf, S (1984) *A Multifactor Model of Deviant Sexuality*, paper presented at 3rd International Conference on Victimology, Lisbon.
[49] Finkelhor, D (1984) *Child Sexual Abuse: New Theory & Research*, New York, Free Press.
[50] Prentky, R (1995) A Rationale for the Treatment of Sex Offenders: Pro Bono Publico, pp 155-172 in McGuire, J (ed) *What Works: Reducing Reoffending-guidelines from research and practice*, Chichester: John Wiley and Sons.

Figure 1: Wolf's Cycle of Offending[51]

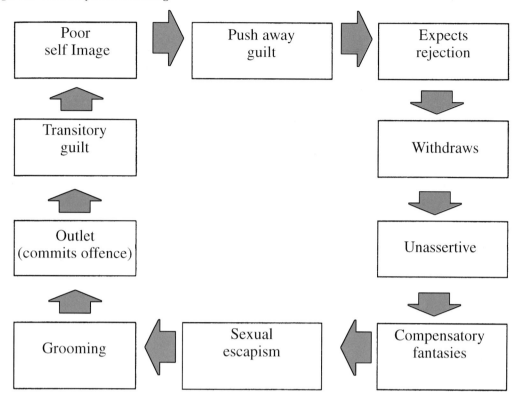

42   The developmental and learning theories developed by Marshall and Barbaree and by Wolf do not distinguish between types of offender. However, the theory developed by Finkelhor analyses why and how offenders commit sexual offences against children. His theory explains why adults become sexually interested in children and provides a model of the process by which an offence is committed (see Figure 2 below). Finkelhor maintains that adult sexual interest in children is based on:

- the emotional congruence that child abusers have with children;

- a predisposition to find children sexually arousing;

- the inability to meet sexual and emotional needs in appropriate consenting adult relationships;

- the failure, or absence, of normal inhibitions against having sexual contact with children.

43   The model of the offending process has four stages which describe the necessary preconditions for the perpetration of an offence.

- First, there must be the **motivation to abuse sexually.** This arises from a number of sources and mirrors Wolf's development of patterns of deviant sexual arousal.

- Secondly, **internal inhibitions must be overcome.** Finkelhor suggests that many individuals who find deviant sexual activity arousing are prevented from offending by inhibitions. Most sex offenders recognise that their abusive behaviour is illegal, but have overcome inhibitions which prevent them from offending. The process of

---

[51] From Fisher, D (1994) Sex Offenders: Who are they? Why are they?, in Morrison, T, Erooga, M, and Beckett, R (eds) *Sexual Offenders Against Children: practice, management and policy*, London: Routledge.

overcoming these inhibitions is sometimes aided by the use of alcohol or drugs as disinhibitors and may involve distorted thinking.

- Thirdly, **external inhibitions or controls must be overcome**. This may involve strategies to gain unsupervised access to a child.

- Fourthly, **the resistance of the child victim must be overcome.** As with the third precondition, this stage forms part of the planning process by the offender and includes the choosing and the grooming of the victim. Examples of this stage include developing a friendship with the child, or inducing and coercing the child.

Figure 2: Finkelhor's Four Preconditions[52]

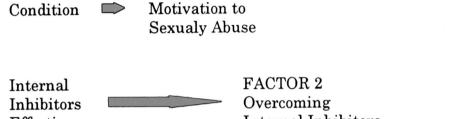

No abuse
Condition ⇨ FACTOR 1
Motivation to
Sexualy Abuse

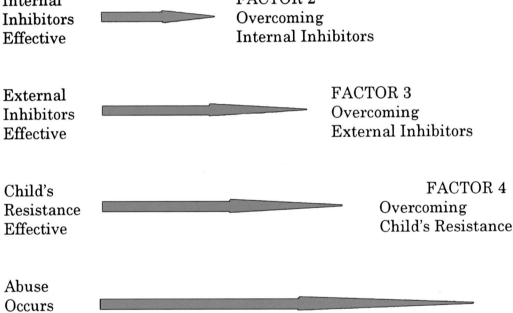

Internal
Inhibitors
Effective

FACTOR 2
Overcoming
Internal Inhibitors

External
Inhibitors
Effective

FACTOR 3
Overcoming
External Inhibitors

Child's
Resistance
Effective

FACTOR 4
Overcoming
Child's Resistance

Abuse
Occurs

44   As in Wolf's approach, the theory developed by Prentky identifies aspects of childhood experience and factors in an individual's adult life which are associated with perpetration of sexual assault. The following factors, although not necessarily present in all cases, are associated with sex offenders:

- **impaired relationships with adults,** due to poor social and interpersonal skills;

- **lack of victim empathy or understanding of the victim's experience or perspective.** This is common in all offenders involved in interpersonal violence;

- **degree and nature of anger,** with a distinction being made between instrumental

---

[52] Figure adapted by Gerrilyn Smith in O'Callaghan, D and Print, B (1994) Adolescent Sexual Abusers: research, assessment and treatment, in Morrison, T, Erooga, M and Beckett, R (eds) *Sexual Offenders Against children: practice, management and policy*, London: Routledge.

aggression (i.e. the amount necessary to gain victim compliance) and expressive aggression (i.e. an amount which exceeds the instrumental level);

- **cognitive distortions,** which are ideas, thoughts and attitudes that deny, minimise, trivialise, or attempt to justify offending behaviour. They are thought to have been learned in childhood and reinforced through adolescence and adulthood;

- **sexual fantasy and deviant sexual arousal**, although research has not yet concluded that sex offenders necessarily have more deviant fantasies than non offenders; and

- **antisocial personality/lifestyle impulsivity**. Child sex offenders are known to plan their offending and engineer situations which provide the opportunity to offend. Psychopathy may also be a factor in some cases.

45   Integrated theories of sex offending have been developed on the basis of experience and study of sex offenders in clinical settings, and have been tested on different samples. These approaches have gone some way in exploring the underlying causes of sex offending and in describing how offenders plan and carry out their offending.

Dealing With Sex Offenders

46   There is a growing body of research which examines the effectiveness of work with sex offenders. The underlying rationale of virtually all the approaches to treatment of sex offenders is the prevention of further sex offending. More recently, advocates of treatment for sex offenders have cited cost/benefit arguments to justify treating this group of offenders[53].

47   Early treatment of sex offenders from the 1950s and throughout the 1960s was based on medical intervention, including psychosurgery (to remove the parts of the brain considered to govern sexual activity), physical and chemical castration, and the use of drugs to alter patterns of sexual arousal. Psychosurgical intervention proved unsuccessful in reducing recidivism and was considered to be ethically questionable[54]. Physical castration has been associated with very low reconviction rates for sex offences; however, studies of castrated sex offenders include men whose offences consisted of consensual homosexual acts and reconviction rates for castrated rapists and child sex offenders remain uncertain. Reconviction rates for castrated sex offenders for non-sex offences were found to be higher than for comparable sex offenders who were not castrated[55]. Castration has now been largely abandoned[56].

48   The use of therapeutic interventions, including psychoanalysis of sex offenders was also a feature of treatment for sex offenders up until the 1970s. Evidence shows that psychoanalysis was rarely found to be effective in reducing sex offending[57]. During the 1970s, surgical and psychoanalytical treatment of sex offenders was increasingly replaced by the use of drugs, particularly antiandrogens, to control sexual behaviour. Sex offending

---

[53] Prentky, R (1995) A Rationale for the Treatment of Sex Offenders: Pro Bono Publico, pp 155-173 in McGuire, J (ed) *What Works: Reducing Reoffending-guidelines from research and practice*, Chichester: John Wiley and Sons.
[54] Barker, M and Morgan, R (1993) *Sex Offenders: a framework for the evaluation of community-based treatment*, London: Home Office.
[55] Sturup, G K (1968) Treatment of sexual offenders in Herstedvester, Denmark: the rapists, Acta Psychiatrica Scandinavica 44 (Supplement 204).
[56] Marshall, WL, Jones, R, Ward, T, Johnston, P and Barbaree, H E (1991) *Treatment Outcome with Sex Offenders*, Clinical Psychology Review, Vol 11, pp 465-485.
[57] Thornton, P (1992) Long-term outcome of sex offender treatment, paper presented at 3rd European Conference on Psychology and the Law, Oxford.

became increasingly viewed as less of a psychiatric condition, fewer sex offenders were diagnosed as mentally ill, and any mental problems sex offenders had were less likely to be seen as related to the offending behaviour. The North American literature indicates that by the 1980s, consistent with interventions for other types of offenders, most sex offender treatment was based on cognitive-behavioural programmes[58].

Elements of programmes

49   Cognitive-behavioural programmes were introduced on the basis of the multi-factoral theories of sex offending that were developed through research in clinical settings[59]. Most UK programmes date from the early 1990s. It is clear that this approach has been used in a number of different ways, in a variety of different settings and with different types of sex offenders[60]. The term cognitive-behavioural covers a wide range of possible components of treatment, but Beckett[61] notes that most programmes in the UK focus on 4 main elements of work with sex offenders:

- altering patterns of deviant arousal;
- correcting distorted thinking;
- increasing social competence; and,
- educating offenders about both the effects of sexual abuse and theories of offending cycles.

Proctor[62] found that the most common goals of programmes delivered[63] by the probation service in England and Wales were:

- victim empathy;
- controlling sexual arousal;
- reducing denial; and,
- improving family relationships.

50   Research has identified 2 key issues in treating sex offenders. These are: amenability of offenders to treatment; and the timing of intervention and of delivering programme components.

Amenability to treatment

51   Studies highlight the importance of sex offenders' attitude towards treatment. However, it is important to note that offenders do not remain permanently at any one stage in the process of dealing with their offending behaviour. While studies tend to examine offenders at a single point in time, programmes themselves recognise that offending

---

[58] Marshall, W L, Jones, R, Ward, T, Johnston, P and Barbaree, H E (1991) *Treatment Outcome with Sex Offenders*, Clinical Psychology Review, Vol 11, pp 465-485.

[59] Salter, A (1988) *Treating Child Sex Offenders and Victims: a practical guide*, California: Sage.

[60] Barker, M and Morgan, R (1993) *Sex Offenders: a framework for the evaluation of community-based treatment*, London: Home Office; and Proctor, E (1996) Community Based Interventions with Sex Offenders Organised by the Probation Service- A Survey of Current Practice, Association of Chief Officers of Probation (ACOP).

[61] Beckett, R (1994) Cognitive-behavioural Treatment of Sex Offenders, in Morrison, T, Erooga, M, Beckett, R (1994) *Sexual Offending Against Children: assessment and treatment of male abusers*, London: Routledge.

[62] Proctor, E (1996) Community Based Interventions with Sex Offenders Organised by the Probation Service- A Survey of Current Practice, Association of Chief Officers of Probation (ACOP).

[63] Beckett R (1994) Cognitive-behavioural Treatment of Sex Offenders in Morrison T, Erooga, M, Beckett, R (eds) *Sexual Offending Against Children: assessment and treatment of male abusers*, London: Routledge.

behaviour and attitutes towards it are not static: offenders' attitudes are dynamic and are subject to change over time. In their study of child sex abusers, Waterhouse et al[64] found that certain patterns of offending may be more difficult to change than others because of their seriousness and duration. For example, they note that high intensity patterns (involving penetrative sex and violence, a long history of offending and more than one victim) are likely to be more intractable. They identified four factors which they suggest might influence whether an offender is more or less amenable to treatment:

- the nature of the offence;

- the acceptance of responsibility;

- the motivation to change; and,

- the type of offender.

This is consistent with other studies[65].

52   Relative success of programmes will also depend on the assessed degree of risk an offender poses [66] and length and intensity of treament. Effective treatment may require considerable resources, for example intervention for some offenders may require long term, intensive specialist therapy in residential settings, and would require fully trained staff.[67]

Timing

53   Research suggests that the timing of interventions with sex offenders needs to be an integral part of programme design. This is seen as particularly important since sex offenders often deny that they have committed an offence or minimise the extent of their offending behaviour. Some offenders continue to deny their guilt even after conviction. Research suggests that attempting to challenge sex offenders' beliefs about the impact of their offending behaviour before they are able to cope with the recognition of what they have done may push them further into denial and minimisation and reduce the development of victim empathy, which is necessary for effective treatment[68].

54   In addition, some studies highlight the need to ensure that attempting to increase victim empathy in sex offenders does not provide them with material or images that they find sexually arousing. In equipping sex offenders with increased social skills, practitioners need to ensure that they do not enhance offenders' ability to become more accomplished in perpetrating and concealing their offences.

---

[64] Waterhouse, L, Dobash, R and Carnie, J (1994) *Child Sexual Abusers*, The Scottish Office Central Research Unit: Edinburgh.
[65] See, for example, McGrath, R (1991) Sex Offender Risk Assessment and Dispositional Planning: A Review of Empirical and Clinical findings, International Journal of Offender Therapy Comparative Criminology 35(4), pp 328-350; and Prentky, R (1995) A Rationale for the Treatment of Sex Offenders: Pro Bono Publico, pp 155-173 in McGuire J (ed) *What Works: Reducing Reoffending - guidelines from research and practice*, Chichester: John Wiley & Sons.
[66] Beech, A, Beckett, R, Fisher, D and Fordham, A (1994) *Community-based treatment for sex offenders: an evaluation of seven treatment programmes*, London: Home Office.
[67] Cook, D, Fox, C, Weaver, C, Rooth, G (1991) *The Berkeley Group: Ten Years' Experience of a Group for Non-Violent Sex Offenders*, British Journal of Psychiatry, 158, pp 238-24.
[68] Beech, A, Beckett, R, Fisher, D and Fordham, A (1994) *Community-based treatment for sex offenders: an evaluation of seven treatment programmes*, London: Home Office.

Effectiveness of programmes

55   The development of cognitive-behavioural programmes has been based on evidence from studies of effectiveness with sex offenders and therefore there are reasons to be cautiously optimistic about the value of such programmes. However, the literature on effectiveness of work with sex offenders is not extensive and different research methods result in differences in the levels of confidence that can be attached to the findings. Further, evaluations of programmes using cognitive-behavioural treatment deal with small numbers of different types of sex offenders who have diverse characteristics and whose offences cover a range of seriousness.

56   Evaluations do not adopt a common framework and sample sizes and type are usually restricted to those sex offenders already selected for programme participation. The basis of this selection may often be skewed by the targeting of certain sex offenders for treatment, for example those with previous offending histories or those who are imprisoned. Few studies compare outcomes with those for a control group of untreated offenders[69]. Where reconviction rates are used in evaluation, the length of follow-up and the type of reconviction offence counted vary between studies. Consequently knowledge of how effective such programmes are remains uncertain.

57   Stronger evidence about effectiveness would require samples from a number of studies to be combined in order to obtain recidivism rates for large samples of treated sex offenders. Research would also need to include adequate comparisons of recidivism rates for non-treated samples. Some authors[70] argue that insufficient research of this nature has been conducted therefore we do not have sound evidence of effectiveness. Nevertheless, it is widely accepted in the literature that this does not mean that we cannot draw some limited conclusions about the effectiveness of programmes for sex offenders. Narrative reviews which draw conclusions about effectiveness based on analysis of the features and outcomes of different treatment programmes can provide some evidence about the success or otherwise of cognitive-behavioural programmes in treating sex offenders.

58   In their review of the efficacy of programmes for sex offenders in Europe and North America, Barker and Morgan[71] concluded that the cognitive-behavioural model was the most promising. They highlighted the ad-hoc nature of programme development and suggest that this approach evolved in recognition of the lack of knowledge of which elements of programmes are most effective. They found that, given the present evidence of effectiveness and the current state of theory, a flexible approach to work with sex offenders, based on a core of cognitive-behavioural work, is likely to prove most successful. Similar reviews of the efficacy of treatment programmes[72] have reached the same broad conclusion.

59   An ongoing Home Office commissioned study[73] to evaluate community-based

---

[69] Marshall, W L, Jones, R, Ward, T, Johnston, P and Barbaree, H E (1991) *Treatment Outcome with Sex Offenders*, Clinical Psychology Review, Vol 11, pp 465-485.

[70] See, for example, Quinsey, V L, Harris, G T, Rice, M E and La Lumiere, M L (1993) Assessing Treatment Efficacy in Outcome Studies of Sex Offenders, Journal of Interpersonal Violence, Vol 8 No 4 December.

[71] Barker, M and Morgan, R (1993) *Sex Offenders: A Framework for the Evaluation of Community-based Treatment*, London: Home Office.

[72] See Prentky, R (1995) A Rationale for the Treatment of Sex Offenders: Pro Bono Publico, pp 155-173 in McGuire J (ed) *What Works: Reducing Reoffending- guidelines from research and practice*, Chichester: John Wiley & Sons; and Marshall, W L, Jones, R, Ward, T, Johnston, P and Barbaree, H E (1991) *Treatment Outcome with Sex Offenders*, Clinical Psychology Review, Vol 11, pp 465-485.

[73] Hedderman, C and Sugg, D (1996) *Does Treating Sex Offenders Reduce Sex Offending?*, Home Office Research and Statistics Directorate, Research Findings No. 45, October 1996; and Beech, A, Beckett, R, Fisher, D and Fordham, A (1994) *Community-based treatment for sex offenders: an evaluation of seven treatment programmes*, London: Home Office.

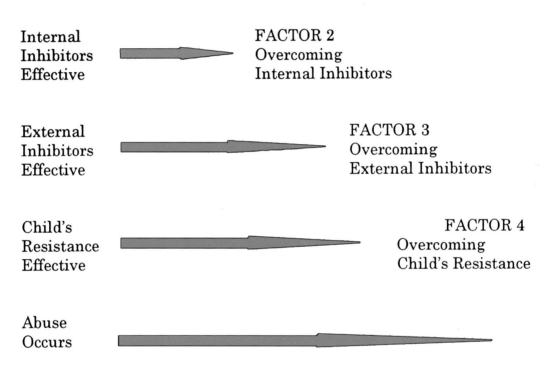

treatment programmes in England and Wales suggests that treatment has a positive effect on both offenders' attitudes and also on recidivism. Child sex offenders are the only type of sex offender for which results are available but the evidence to date (after a 2 year follow-up period) indicates that the outcomes are mainly positive. This longitudinal evaluation will continue to follow up the sample after 5 and 10 years[74].

60   Other studies[75] have found that recidivism rates for some offenders on some programmes are greater than for untreated offenders. Some types of offenders appear to respond better to treatment than others. To date, cognitive-behavioural work has not been successful in reducing recidivism among rapists and exhibitionists[76]. Lack of success with some offenders may relate to their own characteristics, such as lack of amenablity to treatment or entrenched behaviour patterns. It may relate to features of programmes, for example premature intervention or inappropriate timing in introducing programme components (see paragraphs 50–52).

61   Other factors may contribute to the levels of success that programmes can achieve in treating sex offenders. Barker and Morgan[77] suggest that lack of success with rapists may be partly due to different attitudes towards offending between different types of sex offenders. These are linked to differences in wider social attitudes towards adult rape and offences against children. Thus, because any sexual relationships between adults and children is contrary to current social mores, most child sex abusers find it difficult to justify their behaviour even using the concept of consent. On the other hand, sexual acts between consenting adults is a social norm. Thus because the concept of consent has more relevance in the identification of rape and sexual assault against adult women, some rapists will find it easier to deny they have committed an offence. Lack of success of cognitive-behavioural programmes with rapists may also be related to programmes' emphasis on individual responsibility, whereas some writers stress the importance of social and structural explanations of sex offending[78].

Summary Of Key Issues Highlighted In The Research

- Sex offences cover a range of behaviours and identification of sex offending is adversely affected by the private nature of offending behaviour and issues of consent.

- Sex offending is under-recorded and is associated with low levels of prosecution for sex offences. Research indicates that sex offending is much more extensive than conviction statistics show.

- Sex offenders are almost always men and they come from all social backgrounds. Although studies of sex offenders have identified that sex offenders have particular

---

[74] The study involved psychometric testing of a small sample (of 59 offenders) from seven community-based treatment programmes for sex offenders. These tests were carried out before and after (or during treatment) to establish deviancy levels of the sex offenders and whether treatment had any impact on them. 88% of the 59 offenders were child sex abusers. A control group of 81 non-offender male adults were also tested.

[75] See, for example, Quinsey, V L, Harris, G T, Rice, M E and La Lumiere, M L (1993) Assessing Treatment Efficacy in Outcome Studies of Sex Offenders, Journal of Interpersonal Violence, Vol 8 No 4 December.

[76] Marshall, W L, Ward, T, Jones, R, Johnson, P and Barbaree, H E (1991) An optimistic evaluation of treatment outcome with sex offenders, Violence Update 17, pp 8-11.

[77] Barker, M and Morgan, R (1993) *Sex Offenders: A Framework for the Evaluation of Community-based Treatment*, London: Home Office.

[78] Darke, J (1990) Sexual Assault: Achieving Power through Humiliation, in Marshall, W L, Laws, D and Barbaree, H E (eds) *Handbook of Sexual Assault*, New York: Plenum.

characteristics, and that these are associated with different types of sex offending behaviour, these characteristics are not specific to sex offenders.

- Current theories of sex offending provide multi-factorial explanations for sex offending behaviour. These theories have been developed from earlier single-factor theories and from experience and study of sex offenders in clinical settings.

- Most treatment programmes for sex offenders are based on cognitive-behavioural interventions. Evaluations of these programmes indicate that this type of work is likely to be the most effective form of intervention with sex offenders, particularly child sex abusers.

Annex to Appendix 1: Sex Offences

What are Sex Offences?

1   The law relating to sex offences is based on a mixture of common law and statutory provisions and is considered to be 'one of the most controversial areas of the criminal law'[1]. The Howard League for Penal Reform[2] noted that:

'[the] law makes no formal distinction between "sexual" offences and other offences. How one differentiates therefore is largely a matter of individual choice, and criteria for classification are open to debate.'

Given the wide variation of offences which can be seen as sexual offences, what is it that makes an offence a 'sexual offence'? A simplistic answer to this could be any offence from which sexual gratification is derived. However, Gane suggests that four behaviours denote sexual offending. These are:

actual or intended violation of another person's sexual integrity;
actual or presumed sexual exploitation of another person;
unacceptable breach of sexual morality by directly or indirectly regulating consensual conduct; or
unacceptable breach of sexual decency.

Review Definition

2   For the purposes of the Review sex offenders are defined by the terms of the Sex Offenders Act 1997 which includes those people convicted of the following offences (subject to exemptions stated in the Act):

Common Law Offences
rape;
clandestine injury to women;
abduction of a woman or girl with intent to rape;
assault with intent to rape or ravish;
indecent assault;
lewd, indecent or libidinous behaviour or practices;
shameless indecency;
sodomy;

Offences under the Customs and Excise Management Act 1979

section 170 (penalty for fraudulent evasion of duty etc.) in relation to goods prohibited to be imported under section 42 of the Customs Consolidation Act 1876 (prohibitions and restrictions);

---

[1] Gane, C (1992) *Sexual Offences*, Scottish Criminal Law and Practice Series, Butterworths, Edinburgh, 1992.
[2] Gane, C (1992) *Sexual Offences*, Scottish Criminal Law and Practice Series, Butterworths, Edinburgh, 1992.

Annex to Appendix 1: Sex Offences

Offences under the Civic Government (Scotland) Act 1982

the taking and distribution of indecent images of children;
the possession of indecent images of children;

Offences under the Criminal Law (Consolidation) (Scotland) Act 1995

incest;
intercourse with a step-child;
intercourse with a child under 16 by person in position of trust;
unlawful intercourse with a girl under 16;
indecent behaviour towards girl between 12 and 16;
abduction of girl under 18 for purposes of unlawful intercourse;
person having parental responsibilities causing or encouraging sexual activity in relation to a girl under 16;
procuration of homosexual acts.

Official Statistics

3   Due to different legislative and common law sources sex offences do not form a separately identifiable group for which to provide statistics. Crimes and offences are coded by The Scottish Office according to a semi-hierarchical classification system within a roughly descending order of seriousness. Although no specific category for sex offences is provided by this system most sex offences fall within the second most serious group of crimes - 'Crimes of Indecency'. Within this category four subgroups can be identified:

Sexual assault (rape, assault with intent to ravish, and indecent assault);

Lewd and libidinous practices (indecent behaviour towards children, shameless indecency, and indecent exposure);

Other offences excluding offences related to prostitution (procuration, unlawful intercourse with girls under 13 and 16, incest, unlawful homosexual acts, and unnatural crimes); and,

Offences related to prostitution

Further sex offences are listed under other crime categories outwith crimes of indecency. These include:

the common law offence of abduction of a woman or a girl with intent to rape;
pornography offences, such as the possession, taking and distribution of indecent images of children; or the handling of obscene material; and
obscene phone calls.

Table 1: Sex Offences.

CRIMES OF VIOLENCE		
CRIME/ OFFENCE CATEGORY (with SOHD* codes)	**STATUTES**	**SECTIONS**
11 Miscellaneous −2 Abduction including abduction of a woman or a girl with intent to rape	Common Law	

*SOHD - Scottish Office Home Department

Table 1—*continued*

CRIMES OF INDECENCY - SEXUAL ASSAULT		
CRIME/ OFFENCE CATEGORY (with SOHD codes)	**STATUTES**	**SECTIONS**
14 Rape	Common Law Criminal Law (Consolidn) (S) Act 1995	7 (3)
15 Assault with intent to Ravish	Common Law	
16 Indecent Assault	Common Law	

CRIMES OF INDECENCY - LEWD AND LIBIDINOUS PRACTICES		
CRIME/ OFFENCE CATEGORY (with SOHD codes)	**STATUTES**	**SECTIONS**
17 Lewd and Libidinous Practices and Indecent Exposure – 1 Lewd and libidinous behaviour towards children, Shameless Indecency	Common Law Criminal Law (Consolidn) (S) Act 1995	6
– 2 Indecent Exposure	Common Law	

OTHER CRIMES OF INDECENCY EXCLUDING OFFENCES RELATED TO PROSTITUTION		
CRIME/ OFFENCE CATEGORY (with SOHD codes)	**STATUTES**	**SECTIONS**
12 Incest	Common Law Criminal Law (Consolidn) (S) Act 1995	1-2
13 Unnatural Crimes – 1 Homosexual Acts	Common Law Criminal Law (Consolidn) (S) Act 1995	13 (5)
– 2 Bestiality	Common Law	
– 3 Assault to commit unnatural crimes	Common Law	
18 Procuration and Other Sexual Offences – 1 Procuration (excluding homosexual acts)	Criminal Law (Consolidn) (S) Act 1995 Mental Health (S) Act 1984	7 (1-2) 106 (1) (b)
– 2 Defilement of girl under 13	Criminal Law (Consolidn) (S) Act 1995	5 (1-2)
– 3 Defilement of girl under 16	Criminal Law (Consolidn) (S) Act 1995	3 5 (3)
– 4 Carnal knowledge of mentally defective or lunatic person	Criminal Justice (S) Act 1980 Mental Health (S) Act 1984	80 (4) 106 (1) (a)
– 5 Householder permitting carnal knowledge of mentally defective	Criminal Law (Consolidn) (S) Act 1995 Mental Health (S) Act 1984	9 106 (1) (c)
– 6 Abducting girl under 18, woman defective or lunatic	Criminal Law (Consolidn) (S) Act 1995	8 (1)
– 7 Brothel Keeping	Criminal Justice (S) Act 1980 Criminal Law (Consolidn) (S) Act 1995	80 (13) 8 (3) 11 (5)
– 8 Person with custody & care of girl or other causing her seduction	Criminal Law (Consolidn) (S) Act 1995 Mental Health (S) Act 1984	10 107
– 9 Immoral Traffic	Criminal Law (Consolidn) (S) Act 1995	11(1,4)13(9)
– 11 Clandestine Injury to women	Common Law	
– 12 Procuration of Homosexual Acts	Criminal Law (Consolidn) (S) Act 1995 Criminal Law (Consolidn) (S) Act 1995	13(5) proc. 13(6)

Annex to Appendix 1: Sex Offences

Table 1—*continued*

OFFENCES RELATED TO PROSTITUTION (CRIMES OF INDECENCY)		
CRIME/ OFFENCE CATEGORY **(with SOHD codes)**	**STATUTES**	**SECTIONS**
18 Procuration and Other Sexual Offences – 10 Offences related to prostitution	Civic Government (S) Act 1982	46

CRIMES OF DISHONESTY		
CRIME/ OFFENCE CATEGORY **(with SOHD codes)**	**STATUTES**	**SECTIONS**
25 Fraud	Customs & Excise Management Act 1979	170

MISCELLANEOUS OFFENCES		
CRIME/ OFFENCE CATEGORY **(with SOHD codes)**	**STATUTES**	**SECTIONS**
47 Disorderly conduct – 2 Breach of the Peace	Common Law Post Office Act 1953 Telecommunications Act 1984	11 (1) (a) 43
59 Obscene Material and Sex Shop Offences – 1 Handling obscene material	Common Law British Telecommunications Act 1981 Children & Young Persons (Harmful Publications) Act 1955 Civic Government (Scotland) Act 1982 Criminal Justice Act 1988 Customs Consolidation Act 1876 Indecent Displays (Control) Act 1981 Judicial Prosecutions (Reg. of Reports) Act 1926 Obscene Publications Acts Post Office Act 1953	49 2 51-52 160 11(1) (b-c)
77 Revenue and Excise Offences (excluding vehicle and drugs)	Customs and Consolidation Act 1876	42

Definitions Of Sex Offences[3]

Sexual Assault

Rape

4 Common law offence of carnal knowledge of female (sexual intercourse) by a male obtained by overcoming her will. The requirement of 'sexual intercourse' or 'carnal knowledge' is satisfied by any degree of penetration of the woman's vagina by the man's penis. This need not be accompanied by emission of semen. Sexual intercourse with a girl under the age of 12, regardless of whether consent has seemingly been given constitutes rape at common law, as girls under 12 lack legal capacity to consent.

Assault with Intent to Rape or Ravish

5 This is an aggravated form of common law assault and is distinguished from attempted rape on the basis that the assault is not sufficiently proximate to a completed rape to amount to an attempt.

Indecent Assault

6 This is a common law assault accompanied by circumstances of indecency. Due to the restricted definition of rape as genital penetration many sexual assaults, which do not involve sexual intercourse or an intention to have forcible sexual intercourse, will be charged as indecent assault or as a form of shameless indecency. Thus the offence encompasses a wide spectrum of conduct ranging from relatively minor offences which may involve annoyance or embarrassment, to serious offences of sexual aggression.

Lewd and Libidinous Practices

Lewd and libidinous behaviour towards children

7 Common law offence of engaging in lewd, indecent and libidinous practices towards girls or boys under the age of puberty (12 years), regardless of whether or not they consent as they lack the legal capacity to consent. Such practices may include indecent handling of the child; however, there is no need for any physical contact between the parties and the offence may be constituted by engaging in indecent conduct in the presence of a child.

It is a statutory offence under the Criminal Consolidation (Scotland) Act 1995 to engage in lewd, indecent or libidinous practice or behaviour towards a girl over 12 and under 16, regardless of whether consent has been given.

Shameless indecency

8 This common law offence covers a broad range of conduct and is recorded in the category of lewd and libidinous practices. The offence may relate to lewd practices with a

---

[3] The information in this section has been taken from:
Gordon, G H (1978) 2nd edition, *The Criminal Law of Scotland*, The Scottish Universities Law Institute, Edinburgh.
Gane, C (1992) *Sexual Offences*, Scottish Criminal Law and Practice Series, Butterworths, Edinburgh.
Criminal Justice Statistics, The Scottish Office Home Department.

child and indecent exposure; however it also extends to the sale or display of obscene articles.

Shameless indecency cases may involve sexual relations, an affront to public decency (i.e. indecent exposure), and conduct not only involving an affront to public decency but which is intended, or likely, to deprave and corrupt public morals (i.e. promoting or presenting an indecent display or performance, or selling (or offering or exposing for sale) indecent and obscene material).

Indecent exposure

9   This is not a distinct offence in Scots law. It may be recorded as a form of lewd practice, or breach of the peace, or shameless indecency. It is accepted that, in certain circumstances, exposing those parts of the body that are usually concealed is a criminal offence. An act of indecent exposure is in itself criminal in two sets of circumstances: where the exposure is a form of sexual gesture or invitation; and where the exposure is made in a public place but without any sexual overtones, for example, 'streaking'.

Other Crimes of Indecency

Incest

10   Statutory offence under sections 1 to 3 of the Criminal Law (Consolidation) (Scotland) Act 1995. Involves sexual intercourse between people related to each other within forbidden degrees of relationship. Sexual intercourse has the same meaning as in rape. The three groups of forbidden relationships include:

   direct ascendants and descendants - i.e. parent and child, grandparent and grandchild.
   persons related in the first degree - i.e. brothers and sisters.
   persons so related that one party is descended in the first and one in the second degree from the common ancestor - i.e. aunts, uncles, nephews and nieces.

Intercourse between step-relations is no longer incestuous. However, it is an offence for a step-parent or former step-parent to have intercourse with a step-child who is either:

   under the age of 21;
   or over the age of 21 and has, at any time before becoming 18, lived in the same household and been treated as a child of the step-parent's family.

It is also an offence for a person over the age of 16 to have sexual intercourse with a child under that age who is a member of the same household as the accused in relation to whom the accused is in a position of trust or authority.

Sodomy

11   Common law offence of 'unnatural carnal connection between male persons' (anal intercourse). Both parties are guilty of the offence if consensual. Sodomy in private between consenting males of legal age (18) was legalised by the Criminal Justice (Scotland) Act 1980.

Unlawful sexual intercourse with a girl under 16 / under 13

12   These two statutory offences are contained in Section 5 of the Criminal Consolidation (Scotland) Act 1995.

Abducting or unlawful detention of a girl under 18 with intent

13   Statutory offence of taking, or causing to be taken, any unmarried girl under the age of 18 years out of the possession, and against the will, of her father or mother, or lawful guardian, with intent that she should have unlawful sexual intercourse with men or a particular man.

Person with custody or care of girl or other parental responsibility causing her seduction

14   Statutory offence of a person having parental responsibility in relation to a girl under 16 years causing or encouraging her:

seduction or prostitution; or
having unlawful sexual intercourse with her; or
indecently assaulting her.

Clandestine injury to women

15   Common law offence of carnal knowledge of a woman who is asleep. It may also apply where the woman has been temporarily rendered incapable of giving or refusing consent. It has recently been accepted that this offence is a form of indecent assault[4].

Procuration of homosexual acts

16   Statutory offence of committing or procuring or attempting to procure the commission of a homosexual act:

otherwise than in private, or
without the consent of both parties to the act; or,
with a man under the age of 18 years.

Offences Against Public Order And Welfare

17   Offences against public order and welfare are not classified as 'Crimes of indecency' in The Scottish Office Home Department classification but may include sexual elements. These are classified within the group 'Miscellaneous offences' and include the following:

Breach of the Peace

18   This includes both common law and statutory offences and may include the sending of a message, or other matter, that is either grossly offensive or of an indecent, obscene, or menacing character. This offence also covers other forms of sexual nuisance where the accused's conduct, although not indecent or aggressive has caused distress or offence to others.

---

[4] Gane C (1992) Sexual Offences, pp 19–20, Scottish Criminal Law and Practice Series, Butterworths, Edinburgh.

Taking of, or possession of, indecent images of children

19   The Civic Government (Scotland)Act 1982, (ss. 52, 52A) makes it an offence to permit to be taken or possess any indecent photograph of a person under the age of 16.

Handling obscene material

20   Section 170 of the Customs and Excise Management Act 1979, in relation to goods prohibited to be imported under section 42 of the Customs Consolidation Act 1876, makes it an offence to acquire possess, carry, remove, deposit , harbour, keep, conceal, or in any way deal with obscene or indecent goods. An indecent or obscene article is defined as of a nature calculated to deprave or corrupt persons open to depraving or corrupting influences. Obscenity in Scots criminal law has so far been confined to sexual obscenity.

Obscene telephone calls

21   The Telecommunications Act 1984 section 43 (1) (a) makes it an offence to send by means of a public telecommunications system a message or other matter that is either grossly offensive, or of indecent, obscene or menacing character.

Other

Abduction of a woman or a girl with intent to rape

22   This common law offence is recorded, together with other abductions, as a Crime of Violence rather than a Crime of Indecency. It may be committed in respect of a child or an adult; however in the case of a girl over 12 it must be shown to have been non-consensual. This offence can be committed by fraud or force.

Scottish Statistics

Sex Offences

23 In 1995, crimes of indecency, which include offences related to prostitution, comprised 1% of all recorded crime. There were 11 crimes of indecency per 10,000 of the population in Scotland. The following information is taken from statistics published by The Scottish Office[5].

Table 1: Crimes of indecency recorded, 1995

Sexual Assault	**1,638**
- Rape	403
- Assault with intent to Ravish	195
- Indecent Assault	1,040
Lewd and libidinous practices	**2,381**
- Lewd and libidinous practices against children	1,118
- Indecent Exposure	1,263
Other	**1,528**
- Incest	58
- Homosexual Acts	104
- Bestiality	1
- Assault with intent to commit unnatural crimes	2
- Procuration (excluding homosexual acts)	10
- Defilement of a girl under 13	31
- Defilement of a girl under 16	252
- Carnal knowledge of mentally defective or lunatic person	2
- Householder permitting carnal knowledge of mentally defective	0
- Abducting girl under 18, woman defective or lunatic	2
- Brothel Keeping	6
- Person with custody & care of girl causing her seduction	0
- Immoral Traffic	4
- Offences related to prostitution	1,046
- Clandestine Injury	7
- Procuration of Homosexual Acts	3
All Crimes of indecency	**5,547**
Crimes of Indecency excluding offences related to prostitution	**4,501**

Table 1.1: Crimes cleared up[6] as percentage of those recorded, 1995

Sexual Assault	66%
Lewd and Libidinous practices	67%
Other	96%
All Crimes of Indecency	**74%**
All Crimes	**35%**

---

[5] Criminal Proceedings in Scottish Courts, 1995, Statistical Bulletin, Criminal Justice Series, CrJ/1997/3, April 1997.
Recorded Crime in Scotland, 1995, Statistical Bulletin, Criminal Justice Services, CrJ/1996/2, April 1996.
[6] In 1995 a crime or offence was regarded as cleared up if one or more offenders was apprehended, cited, warned or traced for it.

Sex Offenders

Table 2: Proceedings against persons accused of crimes of indecency, 1995.

Sexual Assault	**181**	**13%**
Lewd and Libidinous practices	**352**	**24%**
Other	**918**	**63%**
All Crimes of Indecency	**1,451**	**100%**

Table 3: Proceedings where charge proved, 1995.

Sexual assault	134 (74% of all proceedings for s.a.)
Lewd and libidinous practices	293 (83% of all proceedings for l.a.l.p.)
Other	878 (96% of all proceedings for other)
All Crimes of Indecency	**1,305 (90% of all proceedings for c.o.i.)**

Table 3.1: Persons with charge proved by sex, 1995.

	Males		Females	
	Number	% of all charges proved for that offence	Number	% of all charges proved for that offence
Sexual assault	133	99.3%	1	0.8%
Lewd and libidinous practices	292	99.7%	1	0.3%
Other	134	15%	744	85%
All Crimes of Indecency	**559**	**43%**	**746**	**57%**

Table 3.2: Persons with charge proved by age, 1995.

	Under 21		Aged 21-30		Over 30	
	males	females	males	females	males	females
Sexual assault	21	0	38	0	74	1
Lewd and libidinous practices	41	0	70	0	181	1
Other	31	98	39	466	64	180
All Crimes of Indecency	**93**	**98**	**147**	**466**	**319**	**182**

Table 4: Main Penalty where charge proved, crimes of indecency, 1995.

Main Penalty	Number and % of all disposals							
	Sexual Assault		Lewd and libidinous practices		Other		All crimes of indecency	
Custodial sentence	78	58%	111	38%	44	5%	233	18%
Probation	23	17%	71	24%	64	7%	158	12%
Fine	12	9%	64	22%	667	76%	743	57%
Caution*/admonition**	6	4.5%	22	8%	94	11%	122	9%
Community Service Order	7	5.2%	15	5%	7	0.8%	29	2%
Compensation Order	4	3%	2	0.5%	0	0%	6	0.5%
Insanity, guardianship, hospital order	3	2.2%	8	2.5%	1	0.1%	12	0.9%
Absolute discharge***	1	0.8%	0	0%	1	0.1%	2	0.2%
TOTAL	**134**	**100**	**293**	**100**	**878**	**100**	**1305**	**100**

* A court may order an offender to find caution (i.e. a sum of money as a guarantee) for good behaviour over a period of time.
** A court may admonish an offender, 'if it appears to meet the justice of the case.'[7].
Admonition (i.e. no further action) is usually associated with very minor offences or where there are substantial mitigating circumstances.
*** This is a more lenient disposal than admonition where the court is of the opinion, having regard to the circumstances, including the nature of the offence and the character of the offender, that it is inexpedient to inflict punishment and that a probation order is not appropriate'.

Trends

Table 5: Crimes of indecency recorded, 1987-1995.

	1987	1988	1989	1990	1991	1992	1993	1994	1995
SA*	1,383	1,322	1,508	1,458	1,429	1,604	1,626	1,603	1,638
LLP**	2,445	2,384	2,584	2,624	2,618	2,596	2,721	2,655	2,381
Oth***	1,438	1,351	1,650	1,952	1,797	1,950	1,700	1,740	1,528
COI	**5,266**	**5,057**	**5,742**	**6,034**	**5,844**	**6,150**	**6,047**	**5,998**	**5,547**

Table 6: Crimes of indecency cleared up (%), 1987-1995.

	1987	1988	1989	1990	1991	1992	1993	1994	1995
SA*	62	64	62	67	66	63	63	68	66
LLP**	54	52	55	57	55	56	62	65	67
Oth***	98	97	98	97	98	98	97	97	96
COI	**68**	**67**	**69**	**72**	**71**	**71**	**72**	**75**	**74**
All crimes	**34**	**32**	**31**	**30**	**29**	**29**	**31**	**34**	**35**

---

[7] Gane C (1992) *Sexual Offences*, Scottish Criminal Law and Practice Series, Butterworths, Edinburgh, 1992.

Annex to Appendix 1: Sex Offences

Table 7: Persons proceeded against for Crimes of indecency, 1987-1995.

	1987	1988	1989	1990	1991	1992	1993	1994	1995
SA*	227	220	226	233	194	203	229	196	181
LLP**	484	450	438	440	433	363	371	398	352
Oth***	753	694	706	1,152	1,006	995	1,082	992	918
COI	1,464	1,364	1,3701,825		1,633	1,561	1,682	1,586	1,451

* Sexual Assault
** Lewd and Libidinous Practices
*** Other crimes of indecency
COI - Crimes of indecency

Appendix 2: Survey of Community Based Programmes for Sex Offenders

Summary of Findings

1   Fifteen authorities throughout Scotland operate programmes focused on offending behaviour for sex offenders. Last year 299 offenders participated in 18 programmes.

2   Programmes varied in size from working with 2 participants in a year to over 50 participants in the larger projects. Larger specialist projects for this group of offenders are in operation in Dundee, Glasgow and Edinburgh. Some of these take referrals from neighbouring authorities.

3   Programmes for sex offenders in the community are a recent and continuing development in Scotland. The longest established programmes were introduced in 1991. Four of the authorities with no current programmes of their own reported that they are currently reviewing their local procedures for working with sex offenders.

4   The greatest source of referrals to programmes last year were the Courts and participants were most likely to be under conditions of community sentences when referred.

5   Most programmes do not target specific types of offenders and accept people convicted of a variety of sexual offences. Some programmes were viewed as unsuitable for certain groups: 12 programmes indicated that young offenders under 16 are unsuitable for their programmes; 9 programmes viewed offenders with psychiatric problems as either unsuitable or only suitable in some cases; and 8 programmes stated that offenders who are unwilling to co-operate are unsuitable for their programmes.

6   Most programmes are delivered in non-residential community settings, and two are based in both prisons and the community. Most programmes operate on the basis of weekly sessions with offenders. The length of programmes varies from under 20 hours to over 150 hours.

7   All the programmes reported that they use cognitive-behavioural approaches with primary objectives of reducing denial, increasing victim empathy, and improving relapse prevention skills. Programmes reported using a range of methods, including individual and group sessions with offenders and working with offenders' families.

8   Most programmes have not been evaluated; however one of the larger programmes has been evaluated, and three others are currently being, or about to be, evaluated.

Section 1: Community-based Programmes in Scotland

1   A questionnaire to obtain information about the range of programmes currently operating for sex offenders in the community was sent to all local authorities in Scotland.

Survey of Community Based Programmes for Sex Offenders

Authorities were asked to complete a questionnaire for each 'specialist project' operating in their area. Projects may include one or more programmes of work with offenders and programmes were defined as:

'activities which run on a regular basis, are specifically for sex offenders, and work to an agreed set of objectives and principles. Programmes may include individual or group intervention, or both.'

Table 1: Projects and programmes for sex offenders.

Local Authority	Number of Programmes	Number of participants in last year
City of Glasgow	3	100
Edinburgh	1	58
Dundee	1	42
Perth & Kinross	1	18
Aberdeen City*	1	17
Falkirk	1	16
East Ayrshire*	3	12
Scottish Borders*	1	10
Argyll & Bute	1	7
North Lanarkshire	1	7
North Ayrshire*	1	5
East Dunbartonshire	2	4
Moray	1	3
South Ayrshire**	1	not in operation
West Lothian	1	no longer in operation
	20	**299**

* Do not consider work as 'specialist project' as such
** Opened in 1997

2 Responses indicated that most authorities do not have sufficient demand to provide specialist projects for sex offenders; however, many authorities' social work departments operate small-scale programmes for sex offenders under their supervision. Some authorities in neighbouring areas to the larger projects are able to refer sex offenders from their areas to these facilities. For example, one project, based in Edinburgh and jointly funded by the four unitary authorities disaggregated from the former Lothian Region, provides a service for the entire region.

3 Fifteen authorities provided information on a total of 20 programmes in their area. Of these, 18 programmes were in operation last year and worked with 299 participants. One authority had abandoned its programme due to lack of resources and a further authority has commenced a programme this year. 17 of the 19 programmes currently in operation are based solely in the community while the remaining 2 are set both in prison and the community. Several of the authorities with no specific programmes for sex offenders indicated their interest in developing existing services for this group of offenders. Four authorities reported that they are presently reviewing their work in this area.

4 The establishment of community-based programmes for sex offenders is a very recent development. Programmes have been introduced in Scotland over the past few years, with the first programmes established in 1991 (see figure 1 below).

Figure 1: Year of commencement of programmes.

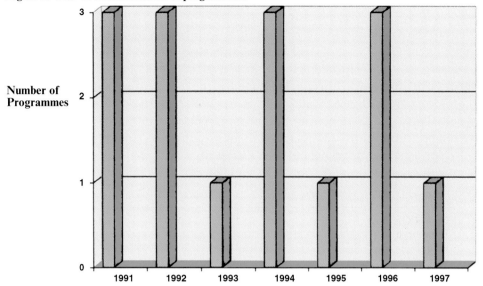

Section 2: The Organisation of Programmes

5   Fourteen of the programmes (70%) are exclusively managed and funded by local authority social work services. However, a young offenders project in Dundee is managed by a voluntary organisation and jointly funded by The Scottish Office. The Integrated Service for Sex Offenders is an equal partnership between social work services and a Healthcare Trust. Other agencies involved in programmes include local health authorities, the Scottish Prison Service and SACRO.

6   The survey found that most programmes are operated by criminal justice social work teams, however a family support team and a homeless team also provide additional programmes for sex offenders in two areas.

7   Usually social workers make assessments about the suitability of offenders for programmes. In the majority of programmes the social worker holding the case or writing the Social Enquiry Report makes the assessment. In only one case, the Integrated Service for Sex Offenders project, does another professional (a psychologist) make these assessments.

8   Programmes are frequently delivered by more than one worker. Most professionals involved in the delivery of programmes are social workers; however three programmes include psychologists in their work and psychiatrists, community psychiatric nurses and residential staff are also involved in individual programmes.

9   Projects may operate more than one type of programme. For example, core programmes for all offenders may be supplemented by specific work tailored to individuals. These may address the special needs of some sex offenders, for example, those with learning disabilities. The larger projects follow core programmes for all participants, in some cases supplemented by individual programmes. Programmes for participants on the smaller projects tend to operate on an individually tailored basis.

Section 3: Programme Aims and Methods of Delivery

10   Figure 2 shows the different aims of programmes and the emphases placed on these aims. Programmes were given a list of twelve aims and asked to indicate which they pursued, and whether these constituted primary or secondary goals. No restriction was specified on the number of goals which could be identified. It is clear that several of the goals form a common core with nearly all programmes including them as either primary or secondary goals. Three goals - increasing victim empathy, reducing denial in the offender, and improving relapse prevention - are included in all programmes. In addition, four goals - the restructuring of distorted beliefs about sexuality, changing sexual fantasies, increasing self esteem/confidence, and improving social skills - are included in at least 90% of programmes.

Figure 2: Aims of programmes.

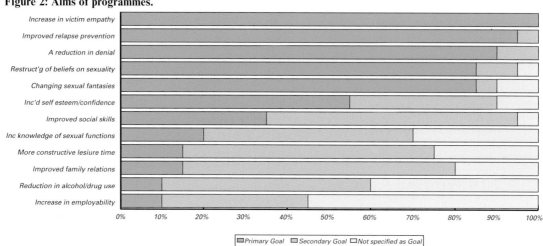

11   In addition to the above aims some programmes identified further aims including the following: increasing the understanding of abuse within a young person's family or by their carer; establishing effective 'safe networks' of support for young people; addressing issues of consent and power; promoting a zero tolerance approach to sex offending; gaining a recognition of the cycle of offending; and motivating offenders to pursue an offence-free lifestyle.

12   The majority of programmes reported using more than one method of delivery (see Figure 3, below). Co-working, where two workers work with one offender, is very common and most programmes operate interventions on an individual basis, some alongside groupwork. Half of the programmes stated that they include working in groups, most of these are either larger projects or programmes set in both prisons and the community. Over half of the programmes indicated that they work with the offender's family and some refer cases to psychologists. None of the programmes reported using physiological intervention methods, for example, hormone therapy.

13   There is considerable variation in reported programme length - from under 20 hours to over 150 hours. Many programmes indicated that the length of individual interventions is determined by the needs of individuals. It appears that these individual elements are often shorter than core programmes for all sex offenders.

14   The frequency of contact in programmes is less varied: most programmes operate weekly sessions. Individually-tailored interventions are clearly more flexible and frequency of contact appears to vary according to the assessed needs of each case.

Figure 3: Methods of programme delivery.

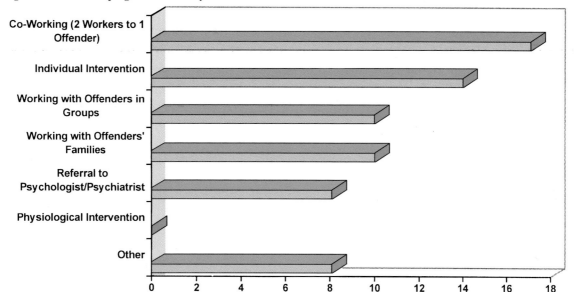

Section 4: Participants in Programmes

15   299 people participated in 18 programmes in the last year. Programmes range in volume of participation from 2 participants to 58 participants over the year. Half of all programmes had under 10 participants in the last year. Table 2 shows that most programmes are small or moderately sized, each working with up to 25 people over the year. However, the 3 largest projects each provided services for over 40 individuals in the last year.

Table 2: Numbers of participants in programmes in the last year.

Numbers of participants by bands	Numbers of Programmes
1 - 10	10
11 - 20	3
21 - 30	2
31 - 40	0
Over 40	3
TOTAL	18*

* 2 programmes were not in operation last year.

16   Most referrals to programmes were made by Courts (47%) followed by social workers (24%). Figure 4 gives sources of referrals from information on 365 referrals made in the last year.

17   Most participants in programmes last year were serving community sentences. Figure 5 indicates the stage in the criminal justice system, or the Children's Hearings system, reached by participants when referred to the programme.

18   Most programmes are not targeted on particular types of sex offenders. However the 4 projects which do focus on particular groups work with young people, usually between the ages of 5 and 18 years; men convicted of child sex offences; and exhibitionists (this last project is no longer in operation).

Figure 4: Sources of referral to programmes.

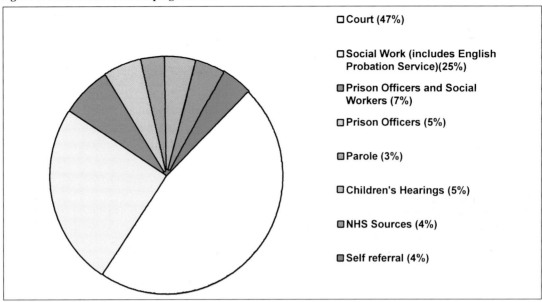

- Court (47%)
- Social Work (includes English Probation Service)(25%)
- Prison Officers and Social Workers (7%)
- Prison Officers (5%)
- Parole (3%)
- Children's Hearings (5%)
- NHS Sources (4%)
- Self referral (4%)

Figure 5: Participants - when referred to programmes.

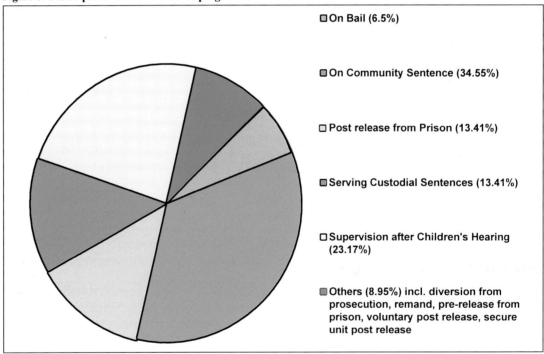

- On Bail (6.5%)
- On Community Sentence (34.55%)
- Post release from Prison (13.41%)
- Serving Custodial Sentences (13.41%)
- Supervision after Children's Hearing (23.17%)
- Others (8.95%) incl. diversion from prosecution, remand, pre-release from prison, voluntary post release, secure unit post release

19   Table 3 shows the wide range of behaviours addressed and the types of offenders accepted by programmes. Programmes were given a list of 10 types of offenders and asked to identify which would be accepted onto their programme. It appears that most programmes will not differentiate between types of offences committed by participants when deciding whether or not to accept referrals. However, for those programmes which do differentiate, responses suggest that men convicted of child pornography offences or who make indecent or abusive telephone calls are less likely to be accepted on programmes.

Additional types of offenders cited by some programmes as suitable included voyeurs and any other Schedule 1 offenders.[1]

Table 3: Acceptability of participants into programmes by type of sex offender.

Type of Offender	Numbers of Programmes	
	Yes	No
Men who rape or indecently assault women	14	6
Men who sexually abuse other people's children	17	3
Men who sexually abuse their own children	16	4
Men who indecently expose themselves	16	4
Men who are convicted of child pornography offences	12	8
Men who make indecent or abusive telephone calls	12	8
Women who sexually abuse children	14	6
Men who rape or indecently assault other men	13	7
Young people under 18 who sexually abuse children	15	5
Young people under 18 who rape or indecently assault women	13	7
Other	5	15

20   Most programmes work with adult sex offenders and have a specified minimum age for participants of 16, 17 or 18 years. Most programmes do not see offenders aged under 16 as suitable for participation. Three programmes stated that there is no minimum age for participants and one had a minimum age of 5 years.

21   In general, programmes indicated that most groups of people with special needs are suitable for inclusion, with the exception of children under 16 (Table 4). Programmes were generally seen as suitable for people with learning disabilities and other mental health problems. Fewer programmes viewed people with psychiatric problems as suitable, and often participation for this group will depend on individual case assessments. Only 2 programmes indicated that females were not suitable participants. There is less uniformity in programmes' acceptance of people who are unwilling to co-operate. While most programmes indicated that offenders in this group are suitable for their programme, some noted that referrals for this group would be conditional on changing attitudes and decisions to intervene would be reviewed.

Table 4: Suitability of People for Programme.

Offenders	Suitability				
	Yes	No	In some cases	No answer	Total
People with learning disabilities	17	2	1	0	20
People with psychiatric problems	10	5	4	1	20
People with other mental health problems	14	3	2	1	20
Young people aged 16 to 18	19	1	0	0	20
Young people under 16 years old	7	12	1	0	20
Females	18	2	0	0	20
People unwilling to co-operate	11[2]	8	0	1	20

---

[1] Schedule 1 offenders convicted of offences against children, including sexual and physical abuse.
[2] Responses indicated that they would work with this group only subject to review and conditional on progress.

Section 5: Evaluations of Programmes

22   Most programmes have not been evaluated. Four of the larger projects have either been, or are currently in the process of being, evaluated.

- A project for young sex offenders was evaluated by researchers commissioned by the Social Work Services Group and the partner voluntary organisation, and the study was published earlier this year. This descriptive study examined the Project's approach, procedures, clientele, and methods of assessing risk.

- The Tay Project is presently being evaluated and this is expected to be completed by the end of the year. The study is examining the operation of the Project and the attitudes and confidence levels of users of the service. It is not known when the evaluation will be available.

- The Social Work Services Group together with the Scottish Prison Service has recently commissioned an evaluation of a project in Glasgow, which will begin in November 1997 and continue until May 1999. The study will involve an examination of the operation of the project and report on a follow up of participants.

- An evaluation of the Edinburgh based project (jointly funded by the NHS Trust and the local social work department) is currently being undertaken. This evaluation includes a descriptive report, based primarily on a survey of workers, and the planned completion date is November 1997.

Annex to Appendix 2: Location of Personal Change Programmes

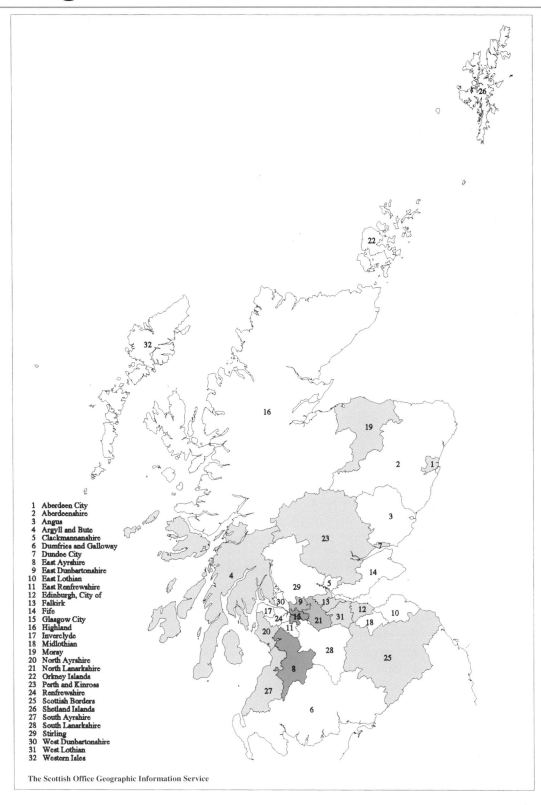

1 Aberdeen City
2 Aberdeenshire
3 Angus
4 Argyll and Bute
5 Clackmannanshire
6 Dumfries and Galloway
7 Dundee City
8 East Ayrshire
9 East Dunbartonshire
10 East Lothian
11 East Renfrewshire
12 Edinburgh, City of
13 Falkirk
14 Fife
15 Glasgow City
16 Highland
17 Inverclyde
18 Midlothian
19 Moray
20 North Ayrshire
21 North Lanarkshire
22 Orkney Islands
23 Perth and Kinross
24 Renfrewshire
25 Scottish Borders
26 Shetland Islands
27 South Ayrshire
28 South Lanarkshire
29 Stirling
30 West Dunbartonshire
31 West Lothian
32 Western Isles

The Scottish Office Geographic Information Service

Glossary[1]

Admonition	court disposal in which the offender is given a warning. It is recorded as a conviction.
Action plan	plan made by supervising social worker for work with offender which may include both supervision and personal change elements.
Adult offender	legal classification of offender aged 21 or over.
Bail	in criminal proceedings, bail acts as a form of security when a person charged with a crime or offence is released before the trial takes place.
Care Programme Approach (CPA)	approach to working with people with severe and enduring mental illness who also have complex health and social care needs, which aims to ensure that they receive ongoing care and supervision in the community when they are discharged from hospital.
Case conference	where a number of professionals meet to discuss a case that is of concern. Frequently used in child protection cases.
Child	legal classification of person aged under 16 (or under 18 with a current supervision requirement from a children's hearing).
Child Assessment Order	provision contained in the Children (Scotland) Act 1995 which enables social workers to obtain a court order authorising access to children for assessment when parents refuse to co-operate.
Child pornography offences	statutory offences defined in sections 52 and 52A of the Civic Government (Scotland) Act 1982 as offences of the taking, distribution, or possession of indecent photographs of persons under the age of 16.
Child protection cases	procedures including inquiries, case conferences, and supervision by social work services, to protect children who are identified as 'at risk'.
Child Protection Order (CPO)	Sheriff court disposal, introduced in the Children (Scotland) Act 1995 which enables local authorities to place a child temporarily in a place of safety when a child is viewed as likely to suffer significant harm and where immediate removal to, or retention in a place of safety is necessary.
Child protection register	register of information about children considered to be 'at risk'.
Children's Hearing (or Children's Panel)	panel of trained lay people to which children who have committed offences, or who are in need of care and protection can be referred. The Hearing considers the child's behaviour or problems and needs, with professionals and families, and makes decisions about what action to take.

---

[1] This glossary has drawn on the following sources:
Young P (1997) *Crime and Criminal Justice in Scotland*, The Scottish Office Central Research Unit, Edinburgh: The Stationary Office.
Morrison T, Erooga M, Beckett R (Eds.) (1994) *Sexual Offending Against Children: assessment and treatment of male abusers*, London: Routledge.

Civil Law	the law which is concerned with the rights and duties of legal or private persons and with settling disputes between people.
Clear-up rates	the police consider a crime or offence to be 'cleared up' if there is a sufficiency of evidence under Scots law, to justify consideration of criminal proceedings.
Cognitive behavioural approach	approach used in personal change programmes which addresses offenders' distorted perceptions about their behaviour and seeks to help them to face up to the consequences of their actions, understand their motives, and develop new ways of controlling their behaviour.
Community Care Order (CCO)	the Mental Health (Patients in the Community) Act 1995 introduced this order to ensure that mentally disordered people who are no longer ill enough to be detained in hospital, but who may find it difficult to cope in the community without special support, receive the medical treatment and after-care services to which they are entitled. The order may include conditions making the person live in a particular place or attend for treatment, education or training.
Community Protection Order	proposed Order which would prohibit convicted sex offenders from visiting specified areas, e.g. school playgrounds.
Community notification	the release of information about identified convicted sex offenders to members of the general public. Information may be passed on to specific members of the public or made available to the general public (general notification). Also known as public notification / disclosure.
Community Service Order (CSO)	court disposal requiring an offender to undertake up to 300 hours unpaid work in the community, under the supervision of a social worker.
Compensation Order (CO)	court disposal requiring an offender to pay the victim of his crime for any resulting injury, loss or damage.
Contact offences	those offences were there is physical contact between the offender and victim.
Conviction	a finding of guilty in a criminal court.
Co-working	method of working with offenders using two workers to one offender.
Distorted thinking about sexual behaviour	term used to describe offender's failure to perceive illegal sexual activity as wrong.
Diversion	a Procurator Fiscal can direct offenders away from prosecution where it is not considered to be in the public interest. Diversion can include social work assistance and reparation and mediation schemes.
Entrenched	persistent and enduring patterns of behaviour.
Exclusion Order (EO)	provision contained in section 76 of the Children (Scotland) Act 1995 which enables a Sheriff to make an order excluding any person named in the order from a child's family home.
External inhibitors	conditions in individual's life which act as a control over sexual offending, e.g. a watchful family.

Glossary

Extra-familial sex offences	offences committed by those outside of the family of the victim, including those who have some responsibility for the victim, e.g. baby-sitters, teachers, etc.
Family therapy	method of working with families to improve their functioning.
Groupwork	method used in change programmes in which a group of offenders meet together to undertake the programme.
Guardianship Order (GO)	court disposal where an offender who is suffering from a mental disorder is placed under the control of a guardian.
Heterogeneous	varied sample of people who are unlike each other.
Hospital Order (HO)	court disposal where an offender who is suffering from a mental disorder is detained in a hospital.
Incidence	measure of the number of offences committed and recorded over a period of time.
Indeterminate sentences	sentences without a specified period. Also known as life sentences.
Internal inhibitors	factors relating to an individuals personality which act as a control over sexual offending, e.g. a strong wish not to offend.
Intra-familial sex offences	offences against those related by kinship, a member of the same household, or parental relationship (e.g. including cohabitee or stepfather).
Lewd and libidinous practices	category of sex offences which includes indecent behaviour towards children, shameless indecency and indecent exposure.
Life licence	an offender serving a life sentence may be released on parole by the Secretary of State with the advice of the Parole Board.
Megan's Law	name given to statute introduced in New Jersey in 1994 following the murder of a 7 year-old girl, Megan Kanka, by a convicted sex offender after his release into the community. The law directs law enforcement agencies to notify communities of the whereabouts of convicted sex offenders in their area.
Minimisation	attitude of convicted sex offenders who do not take full responsibility for their offence or acknowledge the full extent of the impact of their behaviour.
Monitoring	routinised arrangements for maintaining up-to-date information about the whereabouts of convicted sex offenders.
Non-contact offences	those where there is no physical contact between the offender and victim, e.g. indecent exposure.
Non-parole licence	an offender given a custodial sentence of 4 years or over, who is not released early on parole, is supervised on non-parole licence on release from prison.
Offence cycle	theoretical model to describe the process by which sex offenders come to offend.

Paedophile	people who have a sexual orientation towards children.
Parole	the discretionary early release of a long-term prisoner on licence and subject to conditions (particularly social work supervision) on the recommendation of the Parole Board for Scotland.
Perpetrator	person who commits sex offences who is not necessarily detected or convicted.
Personal change programmes	programmes, including residential programmes, aimed at helping offenders avoid or eradicate their criminal sexual behaviour through control or management of their drives and feelings in other ways than offending. Programmes may use a range of psychological, psycho-social or other methods, and be provided by social workers, psychologists, doctors or other health professionals, and involve others, such as residential or prison staff.
Personal safety programmes	educational programmes which promote pupils' skills, knowledge and understanding to assist them in living safely and to feel empowered to reject inappropriate behaviours.
Physiological approaches	method of treatment of sex offenders based on a medical approach, for example hormone therapy or castration to reduce sexual offending.
Prevalence	measure of the proportion of victims of sexual offending in the population.
Probation Order (PO)	community disposal which combines supervision and control with help to deal with offence related problems. Probation orders may have additional conditions added to them and can last for between six months and three years.
Procurator Fiscal	public prosecutor who, following the reporting of a crime, decides whether or not to prosecute.
Psychotherapy	treatment of mental disorders by the use of psychological methods.
Public notification	the release of information about identified convicted sex offenders to members of the general public. Information may be passed on to specific members of the public or made available to the general public (general notification). Also known as community notification.
Recidivism	measure of the rate of reoffending by convicted offenders.
Reconviction	a new criminal conviction.
Registration	notification of the local police of an offender's address or any changes of their names or addresses.
Relapse prevention	method used in personal change programmes which helps offenders to recognise offence patterns and prevent reoffending.
Remand	where an accused person is placed in custody or on bail at the start of criminal proceedings.
Reporter to the Children's Panel	person appointed to investigate cases of children referred to him/her, to decide whether a child is in need of compulsory measures of care and whether he/she should be referred to a Children's Hearing.

Glossary

Residential programmes	intensive personal change programmes for offenders operated in specialist residential setting.
Risk assessment	the process of assessing whether someone is likely to offend and how much harm they are likely to cause if they offend.
Risk management	the monitoring and action undertaken to reduce risk of offending.
Schedule 1 Offenders	offenders convicted of offences against children. This includes sexual and physical abuse.
Secure accommodation	residential care with education for young people provided in a secure building that the young person cannot freely leave.
Sexual abuse	actual, or threatened, sexual exploitation of a child or adult victim.
Sexual assault	category of serious sex offences which include rape, assault with intent to ravish, and indecent assault.
Sexual fantasy	thoughts which generate sexual arousal.
Sex offenders (sex offences)	those people convicted of offences involving sexual exploitation or assault. For the purposes of the Review sex offenders are defined by offences listed in the Sex Offenders Act 1997 which include: rape; sexual assault; homosexual assault; lewd, indecent and libidinous behaviour or practices; shameless indecency; and, possession of pornographic images of children under the age of 16 (see annex to Appendix 1).
Social Enquiry Report (SER)	report prepared by social workers for the courts to aid sentencing. It includes an assessment of the offender's personal and social circumstances, the offence and the offender's attitudes to it and the feasibility of a community sentence.
Statutory supervision	where offenders are required by law to be supervised, e.g. probation order, parole, and supervised release order.
Supervised Release Order (SRO)	a court may specify for offenders who are sentenced to between 12 months and 4 years in custody to be placed under supervision on their release. The length of the supervision period will vary according to the length of the sentence.
Supervision and Treatment Order (STO)	a court can make a supervision and treatment order in respect of persons who are unfit to stand trial but who have been found to have committed the Act of which they are charged, or who are acquitted on the grounds that they were insane at the time of the Act. Supervision and treatment may be for any period up to 3 years.
Supervision	planned arrangements for overseeing sex offenders in the community, designed to manage and reduce risk posed by the offender within the framework of a statutory order which may be either a community disposal or a post-custodial requirement. The supervision plan includes an assessment of risk and how the supervisor will check on the activities and circumstances of an offender, monitor compliance with all the requirements of the order (taking action where necessary) and collaborate with other agencies in managing and reducing risk.
Surveillance	the (usually covert) monitoring of the whereabouts and activities of an offender in the community.

Throughcare   social work assistance to prisoners and their families during a prison sentence.

Treatment   medical, psychological, or psycho-social measures following a medical diagnosis that an offender is suffering from an illness or disability that may be remedied or alleviated by such treatment. In all cases treatment is provided by, or under the direction of, a registered medical practitioner.

Victim   child or person who has been abused. Victims are assumed to be of either gender unless specified.

Victim empathy   an offender's recognition and acknowledgement of the impact of sex offences on the victims.

Victim notification   victims may request to be informed when the perpetrator of violent or sexual offences against them is due to be released at the end of their sentence. This applies to sentences of four years or more imposed from 1st April 1997.

Young offender   legal classification of offender aged from 16 to 21.

Printed in Scotland for The Stationery Office Limited
J31143, C60, 12/97, CCN 003808